Change-the-Game.uk

Politics and policies for a modern Britain

Phil Bunker

First published 12th July 2019

Revised 9th August 2019

Revised 11th August 2019

Revised and updated 23rd October 2019

CONTENTS

POLITICS AND POLICIES FOR A MODERN BRITAIN

INTRODUCTION

The 2015 general election, where David Cameron faced Ed Miliband, represented a low point in the quality of our political processes. Policies were announced during television debates that had not been properly thought out. We were expected to compare the parties on the quality of their soundbites. All that has happened since demonstrates the cost of allowing our political parties to behave in this way.

We are living with the consequences. Badly thought out policies generated by a political system that is no longer fit for purpose. You could not run a successful business like this, so why do we allow so many out of date and dysfunctional practices in our Government?

I set up Change the Game ("CTG") after the 2015 election as a project to work through ideas to change and improve our political system. At that time, there were not so many "game changers" as there are today. Now there are game changers in all aspects of our lives. New technology, new thinking, and new ways of doing things are fundamentally improving established industries and institutions everywhere. But where are the competitive forces that will make this happen in politics? Where are the ideas?

To start with, the project was therapy. A place to vent frustration at the strange things that were going on in Government. The project acquired shape and urgency following the EU referendum and the constitutional crisis that followed. The inadequacies of our political processes and institutions were there for all to see. I decided to write this book; to prompt discussion, to put new ideas out there, and to help get things moving in the right direction.

The book's main proposal is constitutional change. It outlines a series of political reforms to improve the system in which our political parties engage and compete with each other. These changes will force existing parties to adapt - and will allow new parties to emerge. The book also outlines a way in which pressure to make political change can be applied. It sketches out a plan for a new type of organisation which people can use to promote those policies they care about. It looks at how the internet might disrupt traditional ways of choosing political candidates and parties.

New political fault lines and ways of doing things are examined and some gaps in the market are identified. Political values are explored and recorded, and a set of policies developed that support these. A process for embedding vision and objectives into a coherent national plan is set out, incorporating the steps commonly used by businesses when preparing strategic plans.

The last part of the book looks at the steps required to make political change happen. Lessons are drawn from the campaigns for political reform in the 19th and early 20th centuries. A modern version of the 19th century Chartists' charter for political change is proposed. The book then considers how our political parties might evolve under this new system.

As the book concludes, it can be seen that it is essentially the foundations of a plan. An ambitious plan to disrupt and improve our tired and out of date political system.

Phil Bunker

23rd October 2019

ACKNOWLEDGEMENTS

There are many people I would like to thank for their assistance in helping me to write this book and in helping me to form my ideas. First thanks must go to my wife, Caroline, for her support and confidence in me over the three years it has taken to produce this book. She has not complained about my late nights and early mornings as I have struggled to wrestle my ideas into words. She has put up with me being present, but not present, as I have lost myself in thought over important national issues - like the absence of street-name signs, and a lack of numbers on houses. She read the first draft of my book and was encouragingly non-judgemental.

I am fortunate to have a large extended family, who have contributed to my thoughts, while wanting to take absolutely no responsibility for this end result. Particular thanks must go to Phil Lambourne and Paul Matthews for their checking of the text. Thanks also go to my grown-up children Alice, Edward, Elizabeth and William for their robust challenge. Thanks also to my brother-in-law Mike Jones who, together with my good friend Alan Wallace, persuaded me to edit out large amounts of "sounding off" that appeared in early drafts.

Thanks, are also due to my sister-in-law, Sandra Lambourne, who was effectively brutal in allowing me to see how some of my comfortable middle-class views would annoy those less fortunate than myself. And a special mention must go to my very bright niece, Stephanie Relf, for giving me detailed written feedback on an early draft. Thankfully, I have an equally bright nephew, Alex Fawcett, who has been invaluable in helping me to bring this book and the accompanying website to fruition.

Beyond family, I must thank my good friends Trevor Patching and Andy Briscoe for telling me to put my ideas at the front, and my biography as an appendix at the back. Writing a book is a humbling process. My colleagues at ABC Investors, John O'Roarke, Paul Cassidy, Peter Horton and Steve Castle have been helpful in providing feedback, encouragement, material and advice. We hold a good cross-section of different political views, which makes for lively political discussions.

The team at Ronin Marketing in Bromley have assisted greatly in their creativity, enthusiasm and challenge.

I must also thank M Owen Clark who, in the Petts Wood Residents Association Magazine, explained how to get a book published. His own book, 2020 Vision, is a unique and interesting read.

1

WHAT IS WRONG WITH OUR POLITICS?

"If you look at the mass of the constituencies, you will see that they are not very interesting people: and perhaps if you look behind the scenes and see the people who manipulate and work the constituencies, you will find that these are yet more uninteresting."

Walter Bagehot, The English Constitution

At school we had a German language teacher called Mr Byron. He was affectionately known as "Bish". He was an elderly eccentric gent that used to smoke his pipe during lessons. Sometimes, he would fall asleep at his desk, gently snoring while we worked. One time, he got cross with one of our class who insisted on waking him up. Bish was on fire. He had put his pipe in his pocket.

Bish taught me little German, but we had the most wonderful political debates in his class. He was an old-school Tory, appalled by the strikes and civil unrest during the 1970's and the militant version of socialism that was in vogue at the time. During the power cuts and the rubbish collection strikes it did seem that the country was ungovernable and self-destructing. I argued the socialist viewpoint, to get the best out of him, and to keep the debate going. I much preferred politics to German. But at home, in Hastings, my parents were both Liberals. Here, I would argue the Conservative case, to annoy my father. I remember, come election time, the Liberal poster on our front-room window - and the Conservative poster on my bedroom window at the back of the house.

In later life, when I had moved away from home, I joined the Liberal Democrats. The Orpington Liberal Club was not far away from my house and one of my neighbours was a regular fixture, playing keyboards at their jazz evenings. But although the music and the beer were good, that wasn't the reason I joined. I wanted to debate the political issues of the day. To maybe have some small influence, by helping to push forward the ideas in which I believed. My experience of belonging to a political party was disappointing. We talked a lot about local issues, but the one thing that didn't happen was to debate the party's national policies. It was difficult to find out what these were. When I did manage to get someone to talk national politics, I often found that they had a completely different viewpoint to my own. Yet I wasn't sure whether I was in the wrong party, or they were.

As a paying member of a political party I assumed that there would be some form of annual survey where policies were explained, and comment requested. But that never happened. I came to realise that my membership fee gave me no influence. The leaders of the party were not interested in what I wanted to happen. They were interested in getting into power so that they could do what they wanted to happen. My role was to help them get into power, even though I didn't know what they would do with that power if they got it. That seemed like a poor deal to me. This was in the pre-internet days, and well before member pressure groups such as Momentum, but I suspect that my experience is still valid. Parties fear alienating their own membership. For every policy a party has that you agree with and want to support, they are likely to have another one that you don't agree with or don't want to support. They tend to get excited about things that you don't really care about, while often ignoring the things that really matter to you. Disillusioned, I abandoned thoughts of political activism and drifted away from the Liberal Democrats.

I found, to my surprise, that I liked the "New Labour" government of Tony Blair. The new Government seemed modern and vigorous and their policies really were progressive and inclusive. Under New Labour Britain got its mojo back. It was a great time to be British. I also liked the coalition between David Cameron's Conservatives and Nick Clegg's Liberal Democrats. The business-friendly approach of the Conservatives, with the Liberal Democrats to sense-check their policies. It was uplifting to see a coalition pulling together in the national interest. I was disappointed that the Coalition chose to have a referendum on a type of voting reform that would not achieve proportional representation, and that for most people was incomprehensible. The Scottish referendum was also very risky. But apart from these things, so far so good. Each government that our democracy produced was largely right for the times.

Things started to go wrong in 2015. The 2015 general election was an unedifying spectacle. Policy was made on the hoof. David Cameron and Ed Miliband ran the election on sound bites. They looked like they were promoting irresponsible pay-day lending companies, promising all sorts of policies today, not knowing how they could be afforded or enacted tomorrow. Rather than producing another coalition, as had been expected, the 2015 election returned David Cameron's Conservatives with a majority. The Liberal Democrats were reduced from 57 MPs to a mere eight, seemingly punished for working in coalition with the Conservatives. The defeated Labour party replaced Ed Miliband with the left leaning Jeremy Corbyn, elected against the wishes of the majority of Labour MPs. David Cameron then needed to enact his promise to hold an election on EU membership, splitting the country, and the Conservative Party.

These developments fractured the consensus that kept our old political groups intact. There is not only adversarial politics between parties, there is adversarial politics within parties too. From being someone who in the past could have voted for any of the three main political parties, I now don't want to vote for any of them. I am part of a growing club. The club of the politically homeless, as described by David Aaranovitch. "A club for people who look around and see no viable political party to represent their views or their sense of what is best for Britain."

If we live in England, politics is dominated by two monolithic political parties that are old fashioned, unresponsive to customer demand. They are selling products that few people are enthusiastic to buy. If they were companies, then like Woolworths, they would have gone out of business years ago. If we can decide which of these political parties best represents our views, we must then contend with the first-past-the-post voting system. If you live in a solidly

Labour or Conservative constituency, then if you vote for one of the other parties, there is little chance that your chosen candidate will get in. The whole voting process will be a futile waste of time for you. Your vote is worth considerably less than a vote in a marginal constituency. In recent general elections dependable constituencies that always vote one way or another, are ignored. Political activists and heavyweight politicians focus on marginal constituencies. They woo those few people whose votes really do matter.

Our election system also hinders our ability to vote for the best candidate to become our MP. In a marginal constituency there may be a particularly impressive candidate, whose values reflect our own, but dare we vote for that candidate if they are not a member of the party whose policies we support? While in a safe seat, we may find that the dominant party presents us with a candidate that impresses nobody, other than their local selection committee. During elections politicians seem to be making it up as they go along. Policy proposals lack detail. Manifestos are disjointed, rushed, and hard to compare. There is no feeling that you are choosing between carefully prepared plans for governing the country.

Many of our politicians are public school, Oxbridge types, born to rule. Others are political strivers. People who are prepared to invest the necessary hours in political organisations as a route to the sort of power, influence and income that they would be unlikely to achieve in any other way. Not enough of them have management experience. Those people that don't have inside contacts or a privileged background that want to become a politician, will need to invest hours at the coalface of local politics. They will also need to suspend the capability for free thought. Their chosen party will take a dim view of them not supporting all their policies, especially the bad ones.

Those talented and independently minded people that do find their way through the system and into Parliament can find life there very frustrating. They have limited opportunity to shape policy or to vote according to principle. The party whipping system and power structures keep them in line. No matter how much life experience they have had before, they are going to have to start at the bottom. That is unattractive for people that have achieved success and seniority in previous non-political careers. That's one reason that good people are not coming forward in sufficient numbers to run the country.

Much energy is expended by each Member of Parliament in running a help desk for their constituents. Sometimes people need their MP to take up an injustice on their behalf. But this workload can become overwhelming. Our MPs are filling a gap that should be provided by more empowered and responsible local politicians, and by more accountable heads of our public services. Once a candidate is elected, there is no structured and independent reporting of what they do on our behalf in Parliament. We vote for people hoping that they will do what's right for us. But unfortunately, once voted in, some of these people do what is right for them, or for their tribes.

So, there we have it. A party system that is dominated by two antiquated and unattractive political parties; monoliths that are not in tune with modern Britain. An election system which inhibits evolution and the creation of new and fresh competing parties. A system that is disempowering and unfair, giving excessive power to voters in marginal constituencies and massive under-representation for minority parties. A controlling political system that discourages independent thought and does not attract the best people. All of which has led me to write this book.

There is a need for our political system to change, but our politicians are trapped within it. There is little chance that breakaway or new parties will be able to establish themselves. The system does not allow political evolution to occur. This is causing political tension, electorate disillusion and bad government. But these bonds are beginning to weaken. There is a window of opportunity. Both the Conservative and Labour Parties contain factions that bitterly oppose each other. Many of their MPs are unhappier than they have ever been at the behaviour and direction of their parties. Party power has been weakened by policy splits and divisive leadership.

The country needs change to occur. That change can happen if MPs work outside party structures to formulate a cross-party agenda for constitutional change. This book outlines a proposal for what that agenda might contain. It is called The Game Changers' Charter. Supporting an agenda of this nature, call it a new Reform Act if you prefer, will require courage from MPs. Their parties are unlikely to support changes that weaken their hold on power. Those political parties with power are likely to want to protect the system that got them that power. This is the Catch 22 of voting reform.

We can all see that the current system is not working. The only hope we have of changing it is by voting in MPs, from across the political landscape, that are prepared to work together to make this happen. We have seen how powerful MPs can be when they work together in this way. MPs from different parties can form a powerful coalition to force reform.

When individual political parties propose electoral reform, this comes over as self-serving and weak. It looks like they don't think that they can win under the current system. But this will not be the case when individual MPs, from across the full spectrum of the political debate, propose the same change. We need a new charter of political reform. A list of changes that will strengthen the power of the people over the political process. Changes that will make our constitutional safeguards work more effectively. Changes that will allow political evolution to occur. A charter for political change that MPs and candidates from all parties can support.

MPs can be emboldened and encouraged in seeking this change by grass roots pressure and support. A branded internet-based organisation, founded on principles and beliefs, could help make this happen. An organisation that can organise supporters by constituency to form effective lobby groups. An organisation that can help individuals that feel disenfranchised or dissatisfied by the current system to identify and to vote for candidates and parties that support reform. These reforms will disrupt and change our existing political system, allowing new parties to form and old parties to evolve. They will enable new leaders and ideas to emerge. They will force our parties and our government to become more customer-focused, more attuned to the needs of the country.

This book sets out a plan to make this happen. It essentially contains three things. A proposal for constitutional reform, to change how our political system works. A proposal for an internet-based lobby system and organisation that will help achieve this. And a coherent set of values and supporting policies. These policies could be adopted collectively by a party that supports these values, or individually, by any or all of our existing parties.

Alongside these three initiatives are three themes. The first is the importance of vision. Knowing where we want to go as a country and having a plan for how to get there. The second is competence. For government and our public services to become more accountable, business-like and efficient and to embrace new technology and new ways of doing things. The third theme encompasses both sustainability and harmony, and the desire to empower and support individuals and communities to develop their strengths and cohesion. To be the best they can be. The book also examines "Populism", and the new ways in which people are beginning to define their political beliefs.

2

CONSTITUTIONAL REFORM

I am not an advocate for frequent changes in laws and constitutions. But laws and institutions must go hand in hand with the progress of the human mind. As that becomes more developed, more enlightened, as new discoveries are made, new truths discovered and manners and opinions change, with the change of circumstances, institutions must advance also to keep pace with the times. We might as well require a man to wear still the coat which fitted him when a boy as civilized society to remain ever under the regimen of their barbarous ancestors.

Words inscribed on the Thomas Jefferson Memorial, Washington.

Thomas Jefferson, writing all those years back, knew the importance of constitutional reform. Our own history shows that one of Britain's strengths has been the ability to evolve, and sometimes to sweep away and to change, parts of our governance structures that are not working properly. But in recent years, although there have been fundamental changes in some important constitutional areas, we have been too reverential of our institutions. Change has become too difficult. Political parties that win using the current rules are not motivated to change them. Suggested changes to our method of government have provoked outrage, shoulder-shrugs of defeatism, or a lack of interest. As Woodrow Wilson said, "if you want to make enemies, try to change something". Vested interests have won the day, time after time. They gum-up and oppose proposals for reform. So, we live with what we've got.

But new discoveries have been made, new truths discovered, and opinions changed. Our democracy was not designed for a world where communication is instant and ubiquitous. A world where unquestioning deference to hierarchies, class structures and political clans has been replaced by individualism and informed personal decision making. A world where powerful national competitors have emerged that do not take democracy as a given. Now is the time to debate these things. Now is the time to form a plan to re-engineer our democratic institutions and structures. Now is the time to change the rules by which our politicians play this game.

Head of state

Let's start at the top. We need a head of state. The business equivalent is chairman of the board. There is widespread agreement in the UK that this role should be filled by our hereditary monarch. If we had a vote for the role, our monarch would win. The British Royal Family helps to define us as a country. The role of monarch is central to our system of government, although occasionally in our history we have changed the person that occupies this privileged position. Queen Elizabeth has given us stability. We benefit from the wisdom that has accumulated from her continuity through a succession of Governments and Prime Ministers. In today's celebrity culture, most people support and revere the Royal Family. They are valuable ambassadors for our country throughout the world.

One of the strengths of our monarchy is that it has adapted with the times. For example, the removal of the rule that male children take preference in succession. Before our Queen finally steps down or passes away, it would be sensible to quietly discuss some further changes with the future King Charles. We are currently in the possibly unique situation of having three future Kings in waiting: Charles, William and George. Queen Elizabeth should be the last head of state whose number of years in that role are determined solely by their longevity. To be fair both to Charles and William - and to young George too, we should agree in advance retirement dates for each of our next three kings. This will give us, and them, a fair and orderly succession timetable. We should also shape a better-defined job description for our new head of state. A role similar to a non-executive chair of the board in business. This will include some formal controls - and some checks and balances.

The House of Lords

The House of Lords is the last bastion of inherited privilege. It is clearly an anachronism in our modern age. Yet once politicians get into the system, they become seduced by its history, seduced by its grandeur. They lose their appetite for reform. It seems that you need to be outside the system to see it for what it is. Outside of the system to recognise a duty. A duty espoused by Primo Levi, "For righteous men to make war against all undeserved privilege."

We need a second house. It should continue to be an august and dignified institution. But we should make significant changes to what it does, how it operates, and how we choose who represents us within it. In particular, it needs to become more democratic, while not losing the ability to harvest exceptional people with experience of high office. A reformed and respected House of Lords would have both elected and appointed representatives.

There are currently 825 people that are eligible to sit in the House of Lords. A more effective, but equally arbitrary, number could be 250 - the majority elected, the remainder appointed. Ideally, these people would be wise, experienced, proven and accomplished. The elected proportion of the Second House would represent our regions. There are 48 English counties. Each county would elect two representatives, one male (Lord) and one female (Lady). This would make the elected element of the Lords nicely balanced between the sexes and the regions. These will be non-party-political roles. Each term will be for two parliaments. Anyone that can prove ten years of residency in the county will be able to apply. The number of candidates will be reduced through two rounds of internet voting. In this way, one of the county's two representatives will be chosen at each general election from a shortlist decided by internet vote.

The English counties will then take 96 places in the Lords. Scotland, Wales and Northern Ireland will have the remaining 40 elected positions. Given the comparative sizes of populations, they should have 20 representatives between them. The increased number, proportionate to England, reflects their importance to the Union. This will give us a total of 136 elected representatives.

The total of 250 will be reached with 114 appointed roles. Some of these will be political appointments, with allocations to each party based on the size of that party's share of the popular vote; senior politicians that have retired from the House of Commons. The remaining seats will go to those that have held high office. These appointments will be formulaic – e.g. the retiring heads of the Army, the Civil Service, the Bank of England, the FCA, plus representatives from the professions, trade associations, academia, trade unions, the media, and religious groups etc.

Life peerages will be given to those elected or appointed to sit in the Second House – but not to others. These titles will be reserved for those that sit, or have served, in the House of Lords. Hereditary peerages will lapse, such that titles are not passed to the next generation. There will be no titles for spouses. Titles will always be earned, not inherited, and not awarded solely as a result of marriage. Peers will become similar in status to US senators. For example, the Duke and Duchess of Devonshire are unlikely to be married to each other. They will have each acquired their title because they have been elected by the people of Devon to represent them in the House of Lords. From this mandate, they will obtain authority and respect.

The House of Lords will provide non-executive oversight of the House of Commons. Their main power will be the potential to refuse or approve new laws that do not have a democratic mandate. That mandate would be achieved through new proposals explicitly appearing in a party manifesto. New laws should flow from a manifesto which has been considered and voted upon at an election. The Lords will not be bound to agree promises made during elections that are not in manifestos. Before a general election, the Lords will decide the timetable to which party election manifestos are to be produced. They will also determine a common format for these manifestos, to allow easy comparison and sufficient detail. They will ensure that elections are carried out fairly. They will have a fact checking and an assurance role for statistics and assertions made by politicians during elections.

The Lords will agree the financial terms and conditions for members of the House of Commons. This will include a "balanced scorecard" bonus-scheme based on factors such as economic growth, rates of unemployment, hospital waiting times etc. All MPs (Government and Opposition), together with senior civil servants, will be eligible to obtain this bonus – ensuring a congruence of objectives in the national interest. The Lords will also be the main body which receives and discusses internal audit reports on the workings of Government. Ministers will be accountable to the House of Lords for remedial actions. The Lords will have a programme of "deep-dives" into the workings of each Government department. This will put responsible ministers and civil servants under scrutiny. The Lords will be particularly interested in Government efficiency, competence, and processes for identifying and managing risk.

A democratic and independent House of Lords will be able to provide oversight of other independent people and organisations. In particular, committees of the House of Lords can appoint, and review the performance of, the Governor of the Bank of England, the Speaker of the House of Commons, the Electoral Commission, and the Director General of the BBC. They should also review and report on borrowing and the national debt, to ensure that Governments are not funding popular policies in irresponsible ways. Finally, they should control the implementation of recommendations of the Boundary Commission

The House of Commons

Our local MPs should be elected on the basis that we trust them to use their knowledge and wisdom to represent what they think is best for us in Parliament. This is our system of representative democracy. But the party system gets in the way of this. At an election, we might find that the person that most closely matches our views on social issues, is attached to a party with a completely bonkers economic policy. Meanwhile, the party whose economic policies we do support might put up a bombastic candidate that we hate. Surely, we can do better than this.

Once elected, if an independently minded MP does stand up for their own views against their party, they risk deselection, side-lining, or possible career suicide. The party whip system neuters them. MPs are told how to vote by their party. Sarah Woolaston discovered this: "Maybe I was naïve, but I thought the whole point of being an MP was to scrutinise legislation and improve it. Is it a bad thing to have MPs voting for what they think is right?"

The system should change so that we can vote in the best independently minded people to represent us locally, while also being able to choose the best set of policies, as represented by our choice of political party. This is the Additional List System. Under the Additional List System people vote separately for their preferred constituency candidate, and for their preferred political party.

Each candidate will be listed against the party they represent. Voters will put a cross against both the candidate they want, and the party that they decide to support. The two things could be different. For example, Janet Fox might stand for the Green Party and you might vote for her because you know and like her, but you might decide to put your cross in the Liberal Democrat Party box, whose policies you like, but whose candidate you do not like. This will strengthen representative democracy since strong parties fielding weak candidate will be punished.

Constituency MPs will then be selected on a traditional first-past-the-post system. These MPs will be joined in Parliament by additional MPs selected from party lists - according to the proportion of the vote achieved by each party. This system will be similar to the one they have in Germany. As Paul Lever explains in his book, Berlin Rules, the Bundestag has around 630 members. Half of them are directly elected by constituencies on a first-past-the-post basis. The other half are elected from regional party lists - proportionately to the overall number of votes secured by their parties.

There will no longer be any "wasted votes". If your chosen party has no chance of winning in your constituency, you can still vote for it, knowing that this will count towards their list allocation. You will then be able to vote for whichever of the front-running candidates in your constituency that you dislike the least.

We will need to determine how many MPs we should have, and how the numbers will be split between Constituency MPs, and MPs from party lists. The UK currently has 650 MPs. They cannot all fit into the debating chamber. With devolution, there should be fewer. An ample number is 550. Of these, 400 would be constituency MPs and 150 would be MPs from party lists. With this system, if a party got 10% of the party vote, then alongside their share of the first-past-the-post Constituency MPs elected, they would get 15 additional MPs from their list. This hybrid system won't please either those that want a fully proportionate system, or those that want to retain a full first-past-the-post system, but it is a way forward. With more devolved power, our current system is expensive, while not producing representation for a wide enough cross section of different views. This will be better.

A system like this could be tailored by having two lists. The first list could contain each party's constituency candidates that got the largest numbers of votes - but did not get elected. This would give some continuity and a safety net for constituency MPs that have just lost out. People like Michael Portillo and Nick Clegg would have benefited from this. The second, larger list, could be made up of people that don't have the time, inclination, or skillset to perform a constituency MP role - but do have important skills or experience that would be useful to the country. Let's call these "technocrats", although party lists might also contain celebrities and the odd Monster Raving Looney. These lists could also help talented MPs that have lost their constituency due to the reduction in the number of constituencies or due to boundary changes.

Manifestos, party policy and elections

When Theresa May called a snap general election in 2017, with a few weeks to go before the election, we didn't know what each party would have in their manifesto. We did not have time to properly review them, or their parties to shape them, Political debate got in the way of a cool evaluation of policy. The production of the manifestos was rushed. They had been prepared by a tiny subgroup, with little opportunity for open party debate. That is not good enough. These documents are vitally important. They should be each party's business plan for the country. They set the framework against which a Government will be empowered and judged. They are the template against which parties will be compared when it comes to the election. We need rules around how election manifestos are produced and what they contain. The law requires unions to get their members to vote before they strike. The law should also require members of political parties to approve their manifestos before they come before the people. There should also be a structured common timetable and format for their production. This would include headings, and the maximum number of words used in each one. An independent commission of The House of Lords would determine a common structure well in advance of an election. They would then rule on whether this had been achieved, before each party's manifesto was approved for release to the people. This process works much better with a fixed electoral term. Any variation to election dates must be for an exceptional reason. A change of date will need to be agreed upon not only by the Commons, but also by the House of Lords.

Political parties will dislike having their hands tied in this way. But we do not want to give power to political parties. We want to give power to the electorate. In return, we would publicly fund political parties based on their numbers of members, and the number of votes they receive. We would no longer have our political parties engaged in the grubby business of fundraising.

English devolution

The powers delegated to Scotland, together with their strong independence movement, has changed our politics. There is resentment from the English that their own identity is being suppressed. There is also resentment in the regions of the dominance of London. Some believe that in the European vote, given the chance to protest, many voters rebelled against rule from London, as much as they rebelled against rule from the EU. There is undoubtedly a problem. As the Economist notes; "Britain is the most centralised rich country in the world after tiny New Zealand. It is a prisoner of a cult of centralised government that was created in the age of mass production but is increasingly irrelevant in an age of tailoring and customisation. Centralisation is alienating people from their government."

One answer is to give England its own parliament. But there is a large imbalance between the separate countries of the UK. England has a population ten times as large as the population of Scotland. An English parliament would also be dominated by London. It would look too much like a parliament for the UK. Better to split England up into devolved regions, each with its own significant devolved decision-making powers. If we had nine English regions, then on average each would have a similar sized population to Scotland. Each should also have the same devolved powers. This would give more balance to the United Kingdom. With Scotland, Wales and Northern Ireland we would have 12 distinct regions. On average, each region would have the same population as an American state. The other parallel is Germany, which is a federal republic. Its constituting entities are the Lander. West Germany had nine Lander when it combined with East Germany. Since the GDR did not have any Lander, six were created, with Berlin itself becoming a Land. Germany now has 16 Lander. On average, each of these also has the population of an American state.

Nine is the magic number for the creation of English regions. Something like this already exists for use as constituencies in European elections. The concept is not new. Winston Churchill proposed 10 or 12 regional parliaments for the United Kingdom. This was the concept of "Home rule all round" which was discussed as part of the process of granting Irish home rule. In creating nine English regions, rather than create artificial constructs, we should go back to the ancient kingdoms of England for inspiration; the Heptarchy. To give them greater stature we should call them kingdoms, rather than regions. Counties will be grouped together to become kingdoms. Some potential names for these kingdoms drop out easily: London, East Anglia, Wessex, Warwick, Mercia, Yorkshire, and Northumbria. But the South-West corner of England needs some thought. What is now Cornwall used to be the kingdom of Dumnonia which existed for 400 years from the late 4th to 8th centuries. That is not a suitable name for the whole region. For the time being, just for the purposes of this book, we will call this region Dorne. In the South-East corner of England, Kent and Sussex were both kingdoms in their own right, but today Kent will not want to be called Sussex, nor Sussex be called Kent. And Surrey won't want anything to do with either of them. So, for the time being, for the purposes of this book, we will call this region The Shire. Here is a possible grouping of English counties into *The Nine Kingdoms of England*.

1. *London* - effectively already a city state.
2. *East Anglia* - Essex, Suffolk, Norfolk, and Cambridgeshire.
3. *The Shire* - Kent, East Sussex, West Sussex and Surrey.
4. *Dorne* - Cornwall, Devon, Somerset and Dorset.
5. *Wessex* - Gloucestershire, Oxfordshire, Buckinghamshire, Bedford, Hertfordshire, Berkshire, Wiltshire and Hampshire.
6. *Warwick* - Shropshire, Staffordshire, Birmingham, Leicestershire, Rutland, Northamptonshire, Warwickshire, Herefordshire, Worcestershire.
7. *Mercia* - Lincolnshire, Nottinghamshire, Derbyshire, Cheshire, Manchester, Merseyside, Lancashire.
8. *Yorkshire* - North Yorkshire, West Yorkshire, South Yorkshire,

East Riding of Yorkshire

9. *Northumbria* - Cumbria, County Durham, Tyne & Wear, Northumbria.

This splits an England of 55.3m people into 9 separate regions: The Nine Kingdoms of England. Add Scotland's 5.2m people, Wales' 3.1 million people, and Northern Ireland's 1.8m people. That gives a UK of 65.5m people (2017 figures) - split into 12 distinctive regions. Together, we will have a strong position in Europe and the world. We will be a most interesting place. A place bound together by our love of democracy, our common history, and our respect for diversity and freedom. A place of romance and beauty where talented people thrive. A place where I want to live.

To mark this reorganisation of the UK into 12 distinct regions, we could make one small but symbolic name change. Rather than be called The United Kingdom, we could call ourselves The United Kingdoms.

Administration of the devolved English Kingdoms

The English Kingdoms will not replace county councils. English devolution will not be about centralising power or creating expensive parliaments. The purpose of the kingdoms is to give regions greater identity, better planning, more devolved power, and to increase their level of influence with Westminster. An analogy for English devolution should be the merger of businesses. Each business continues to run independently, but the group will start to plan to achieve synergies and cost savings, and to maximise its market position and its buying power. County councils will work together to create a plan for their kingdom. The format for the plan will be common between the kingdoms, focusing on communications, tourism, quality of life, and business development. These plans will be presented for discussion and approval to each kingdom's decision-making forum. These will be made up of the kingdom's elected Westminster MPs and their elected representatives to the Lords. One day a week in Westminster (Friday) will be left clear so that constituency MPs - and each kingdom's elected members of the Lords – can go back to their regions to attend these meetings.

Elected heads for the kingdoms

The position of Mayor of London has proved to be successful and popular. The First Minister for Scotland is also a respected position. Each of the English kingdoms should have a leader to represent them. These will be elected, ideally non-party political, roles. One parallel is the position in the USA of State Governor. A fictional parallel comes from The Game of Thrones. Fans of the series might well embrace Northumbria's elected leader as the new "King in the North" - or perhaps, "Queen in the North" - complete with bearskin and Hadrian's Wall.

The Witan

The Witenagemot, better known as the Witan, was a political institution in Anglo-Saxon England. It operated from before the 7th century until the 11th century. The Witan assembled the land's most powerful and important people to discuss matters of both national and local importance, and to advise the King. With more power devolved to the English regions, we will not need an English parliament. But England should have a way for its regions to make representations to Parliament on issues affecting England as a whole. A Witan could achieve this. A Modern Witan would not advise the king – it would advise the Government. Each of the English Kingdoms would send their elected representatives. These would be their leader and their elected members of the Lords and Commons. The hosting of the Witan would rotate amongst the kingdoms. The Prime Minister and the entire cabinet would attend. The kingdoms would present their plans and their issues to Government. Government would then formally respond to what they had heard.

The K12

We should also have a forum for the leaders of the twelve kingdoms to meet. Charles, when he becomes King, will host and chair the K12. This will be a smaller and more private meeting, like the G20, just for the heads of the twelve UK regions. The agenda will focus on quality of life and protection of the environment. It will focus on the findings of ecological surveys, and also *"The King's Survey"*, a national wellbeing questionnaire. The K12 will have advisory rather

19

than executive powers. They will advise both the Prime Minister and the Monarch. The K12, representing the leaders of each of our kingdoms, will also have a governance role. If the Monarch goes off the rails, and that has happened from time to time in British history, it will be their role to get them back in line. If there was a lack of competence, or a fundamental over-stepping of authority, then this grouping will be responsible for deciding what to do about it.

Northern Ireland

The creation of the English Kingdoms gives an opportunity to look again at the status of Northern Ireland. This used to be part of Ulster, one of the four Irish Kingdoms, alongside Munster, Leinster and Connacht. In 1921 it was partitioned, as three of its nine counties, Donegal, Cavan, and Monaghan voted to join Eire. The other six counties voted to remain in the United Kingdom and became Northern Ireland.

In 1998, The Good Friday Agreement was agreed by voters in both Eire and Northern Ireland. The agreement acknowledged both that the majority of the people of Northern Ireland wished to remain a part of the United Kingdom and that a substantial section of the people of Northern Ireland, and the majority of the people of the island of Ireland, wished to bring about a united Ireland. Both of these views were acknowledged as being legitimate. For the first time, the Irish government accepted in a binding international agreement that Northern Ireland was part of the United Kingdom. The Irish Constitution was also amended to recognise implicitly Northern Ireland as part of the United Kingdom's sovereign territory, conditional upon the consent for a united Ireland from majorities of the people in both jurisdictions on the island.

The future of Northern Ireland is therefore firmly in the hands of the people of Northern Ireland. But rather than be faced with a Brexit-like in or out referendum, that would potentially leave nearly half the population resentful, the formation of kingdoms in England presents an intermediate possibility that could perhaps be voted upon. Forming Northern Ireland into a semi-independent kingdom – attached to both Eire and the UK - seems consistent with the Good Friday Agreement journey. This kingdom could then remain in the Single Market and the Customs Union, passported in by Eire.

Much negotiation and goodwill would be required to shape such a deal. But there are plenty of semi-independent statelets in Europe. Northern Ireland could become the Monaco of the North. The Good Friday Agreement could be followed by the Easter Sunday Agreement, Easter Day being when the really good stuff happened in the Bible.

Scotland

If the UK were a business, one of the highest scoring items on the risk-register would be the potential for the Scottish to vote for and to achieve, independence. That would have a profound impact on the rest of the UK, and on its standing in the world. Just hoping that this won't happen is not an acceptable policy. We need a plan. Brexit gives us the opportunity to think what an Article 50 process would look like for Scottish independence. The starting point, of course, being that we don't want this to happen. We want to keep the Scottish people happy in this Union of ours. We must not be arrogant or inflexible. If the Scottish don't like some aspects of our Union, we should be listening, and be prepared to change. But if it does come to a potential break up, the Brexit negotiations have given us a taste of how this might proceed, and the complexities involved. Nicola Sturgeon has been loud in her condemnation of having a vote on leaving the EU before all of the costs and implications were known. We must make sure that this detailed work is done in advance of any new Scottish referendum. We should start to work on this now. The repayment of our joint public debt is going to be an important issue. We need to work out how much of our public debt would be attributable to Scotland, and how it would be repaid. We should look carefully at the national accounts for an independent Scotland to ascertain whether it would be creditworthy as an independent nation. We also need to talk about defence, and the siting of nuclear assets. We need to talk about unfunded pension commitments. How would a Scottish application to join the EU be regarded? Would Spain veto them because of their concerns over a Catalonia break-away? Would they need to adopt the Euro? What about trade arrangements and tariffs? Would there be a border with England? If nothing else, the Brexit process has been useful in rehearsing all of the issues that will need to be resolved in advance of another Scottish independence referendum.

Nicola Sturgeon also raises an interesting question in her use of Scottish exceptionalism in respect of the UK's EU vote. What, if following a Scottish referendum, Glasgow wants to leave the UK, but Edinburgh doesn't? What happens if the Highlands or the Shetland Islands wants to stay in the UK? Is a vote in Glasgow going to force all parts of Scotland to leave the UK if they don't want to? Should a leave vote require a higher threshold than just a straight majority? While the mechanics of a potential separation are being thought out, the UK Government needs to be surveying the Scottish people, listening to them. Why is it that they don't feel ownership of our Union? What powers would they want under an independent Scotland that they don't have now? What would they want to do with them? Our politicians and our future King need to spend as much time as possible getting in tune with Scotland.

Reduction of the voting age

The changing demographic structure of our country has some important consequences for our politics. There will be proportionately more older voters. In 1974 the over 65s represented 14% of the population. In 2014 this figure was 18%, It is projected to rise to 24% in 2039. And because older people are more likely to vote, they make up a disproportionately large share of voters. Not all old people are wise, generous, and far-sighted. Some have a strong sense of entitlement. They vote to protect their triple-lock pensions and their free bus passes. Meanwhile, many of our young people are struggling.

The numbers of the retired will soon be bolstered by people from my generation; the "me" generation. People that have not been through a war, not done national service, and not bothered to save. A generation that has dined out on a wall of national prosperity fuelled by North Sea oil, increasing property prices, and a vast increase in the National Debt. A generation that plans to keep partying until the grave - and to leave the bill to someone else. That isn't fair. We need to redress the generational balance of political power. We should do this by bringing down the voting age, first to 16, and then lower. A 16-year-old can be as well informed as an 80-year old. They certainly have more stake in the future.

The honours system

Our honours system is opaque. The system rewards time-serving and political cronyism. Private Eye calls it prizes for the privileged "phew" to indicate that something doesn't quite smell right about it. Iain Martin of The Times complains that knighthoods and peerages are "dispensed like sweeties". He notes that the overcrowded House of Lords contains several peers who "would be regarded as too vulgar for inclusion in a downmarket reality television show." Reforming the House of Lords gives us a great opportunity to tidy up and clean up our honours system. It gives us an opportunity to rationalise the different numbers and types of awards - their names - and the titles that go with them. It gives us the opportunity to implement a more transparent and inclusive nomination process

Constitutional reform organisations

A number of organisations are calling for constitutional reform. Lord Lisvane, former Clerk and Chief Executive of the House of Commons, has set up an organisation designed to devise a coherent plan for what should happen after powers are returned from the EU. Their agenda can be found on their website, www.ConstitutionalReformGroup.Co.Uk. A similar project is the think tank, The Project for Modern Democracy, which has produced an initiative called "Governup". The mission of Governup is to analyse the current problems, challenge the terms of debate, and consider the far-reaching reforms needed in Whitehall and beyond to enable more effective and efficient government, with better economic and social outcomes for the British public. The oldest of the constitutional reform pressure groups is The Electoral Reform Society, which was formed 135 years ago. This independent campaigning organisation champions the rights of voters and seeks to build a better democracy in Great Britain and Northern Ireland. The next chapter looks more closely at the activities of think tanks and lobby organisations such as these.

3

DISRUPTION

You rebooted the same old operating system. The same tired old politics of short-termism and self-serving, small thinking, bullshit. I was hoping, praying, that someone, anyone, with a modicum of imagination, could see that there was an opportunity for someone to step in and to make a change.

Brexit: the uncivil war, Channel 4

This quotation is from the Dominic Cummings character, played by Benedict Cumberbatch, in the closing scene of the Channel 4 drama. The quotation illustrates the way that politics is changing, particularly through the use of targeting and new types of communication. During the EU referendum campaign, sophisticated algorithms were used to micro-target populations for political messages and campaigns. This technique was controversial at the time, but it is essentially no different from posting leaflets through doors, just massively more effective.

These new ways of doing things are not going away. Micro-targeting can test how effective ads are - and then improve them in real time. Momentum (the pro Jeremy Corbyn pressure group) produces shareable videos that are spread at almost no cost. It is estimated that one in three Facebook users saw Momentum ads at the 2017 election, even though the group only spent £2,000 on paid Facebook advertising.

This chapter outlines how modern internet technology and techniques can be used to help make political change happen. The modern term is disruption. Disruption is where internet technology enables new organisations to compete with existing organisations on a fundamentally different basis. This has been seen with Amazon and bookstores, Uber and taxis and Airbnb and hotels. How could this happen in politics? The first part of the chapter outlines a high-level plan for a new policy formation and promotion organisation called Change-The-Game.UK. This is shortened to CTG in the text. CTG is also used as an acronym to encompass the wider objectives of the project. The second part of the chapter outlines how comparison websites can be used during elections to help people to choose political parties and candidates. The final part of the chapter looks at how these new types of organisation should be regulated, and how they could fit into the framework for manifestos and elections proposed in the last chapter.

The elevator-pitch

The concept of an elevator-pitch is that if you are in a lift with a potential investor, how do you sell your idea in the time that the lift gets to their floor? The elevator pitch is a good test of both the validity of an idea, and your ability to sell it to others. I began to develop an elevator-pitch for CTG in 2016. I tested it on friends. To start with I was embarrassed about doing this. The conversation would go something like this.

"So, what are you planning to do next Phil?"

"Well, I have a few projects that I want to pursue, some business, some charity, and actually... I am writing a book..."

It was difficult to admit to writing a book. It seems so pretentious. But I couldn't ignore that this was what I was doing. By then, I had invested enough time in it to want to see an end product. Talking about the book with friends would give me that extra bit of pressure to complete it.

"Writing a book, that's interesting. What's it about?"

"Well actually, it's about politics..."

This was the second cringeworthy moment. We try not to talk about politics. We'd rather talk about football. But maybe because of the interesting times we were living in, or maybe because these were friends of mine, they were interested to find out more.

Then I would launch into my elevator-pitch.

"People cannot relate to our political parties anymore. They are out of date. But people still care about politics. They are interested in issues and policies. They need a way to influence politicians to support the things they care about."

I use the example of the right to die.

"People want to be able to make fundamental decisions about their own lives. But did you know that despite huge public support for a change, MPs recently voted by two thirds against any change to the laws on the right to die?"

This gets attention: a nodding of heads.

"There is a gap in the market for a multi-issue pressure group. A branded organisation that will campaign on popular issues, register supporters and their policy interests, and then use the internet to form them into constituency-based pressure groups."

"This will be a new type of political organisation. It will work with MPs from different parties to help form them into coalitions to back specific well worked out policies."

The people I pitched to "got it" pretty much immediately. They were engaged by it. Some of them were involved in direct customer marketing. They understood the customer proposition and the power of a customer database. Having seen disruptive propositions in business, why not in politics?

The plan

Encouraged by this reception, I started to put more detail and thought around the development of a branded lobby organisation and website. An organisation that, amongst other things, could lobby for and develop the reform ideas outlined in the last chapter. To build an organisation like this would need external funding and support. That would only be forthcoming if this was seen as serious endeavour; a force for good. To achieve this would require a plan.

The first part of the plan is the production of this book, together with a simple website to help promote it. The next step is the production of a campaigning website that is not live to the extent of collecting data, but that will show what a branded multi-issue web-based pressure group could look like, and what it could do.

These first two phases build a shop window to help to promote discussion and feedback. After this, if a project like this is to go forward, it will require external funders and a committed team to move it into the third phase, detailed design and build, when a management organisation will need to be established. The IT build will significantly extend the functionality and security of the website – together with producing a compelling smartphone application. After these first three phases are complete, the final phase will be to go live. To start developing and marketing policies - and building a base of supporters to lobby for them. These last two phases are discussed in Chapter nine, Changing the game, in the context of developing public pressure for constitutional and political reform.

An organisation to promote change

The closest parallel to an organisation like CTG is a think tank, combined with an effective lobbying and membership building capability. Wikipedia has a list of over one hundred "British think tanks". This list includes organisations such as The Adam Smith Institute, The Joseph Rowntree Foundation, and The Taxpayer's Alliance. A search on "British Pressure Groups" produces another large list. This includes organisations such as CAMRA, CND and Greenpeace. Finally, "British Political Advocacy Groups" produces a list including organisations such as Cannabis Law Reform, Fathers 4 Justice and Sustrans. This is already a very crowded market. What does the CTG concept have that these organisations do not already cater for? How can CTG achieve stand-out in such an already well-established, and apparently well-funded, market? What would be its Unique Selling Points (USPs)?

The answer to these key questions is that if CTG achieves its aims, many of these types of organisations will be customers and supporters of it, rather than competitors. The ability to glue together a set of policy ideas that people care about under a branded single overriding set of beliefs and principles is something that only political parties could do before. To do this as CTG proposes is new territory. CTG will collaborate with pressure groups, rather than compete with them. It will become a method of validating and achieving the changes that they propose. When working to sharpen policy on the right to die, CTG would naturally want to work with Dignity in Dying. Cycling policy would be worked up with the help of Cycling UK. Electoral reform ideas would be sharpened by the Electoral Reform Society.

In Chapter nine, a historical parallel to the CTG lobby organisation is explored; the nineteenth century Chartist Movement, supported by political unions of like-minded people. CTG reinvents this concept for the modern world. CTG will be a *Modern Political Union;* a new type of organisation, with no legacy, designed with a clear purpose. The customer appeal of a new entrant is not to be underestimated. Neither should be the power of disruption. This will be an organisation designed to be noticed. It will have technology, marketing and communication at its core.

Branding

We will continue to call the new lobby organisation CTG here, but an organisation like this might also benefit from having a consumer brand. For example, *The Policy Shop*, which is a defunct insurance brand. This succinctly explains what the site does. It will be a site where consumers can decide which policies they would like to "buy". Buying in our terms will mean giving their support by adding their name to the lobby group for that policy. It could also mean providing financial support for promoting that policy. Visitors to the shop will decide which policies to take forward and which policies to leave on the shelf. Members of CTG will also be able to propose their own policies.

As well as being a direct to consumer site, CTG will also be a wholesale site. Political parties and individual MPs can use the site to find policies to support, each with a known base of voters prepared to support them. We have seen that the policies that political parties themselves manufacture are often flimsy poor-quality products - that soon fall apart when purchased. CTG policies will be robust creations, fully road-tested and quality checked. If several different political parties and groups of individual MPs support the same policy, that must be a good thing.

Forming policy

The internet is a fabulous resource for discussing and shaping policies. As a mechanism for bringing together interested parties and experts in the same place, it is hard to beat. A well designed and modulated CTG site will be able to produce a high quality of policy examination and debate. CTG will be the place where policy ideas are discussed and sharpened, and networks formed. A site like this can also produce high quality draft legislation. In the computing world there is something called "open source software". Volunteer programmers work collaboratively to produce free to use software to compete with the offerings of dominant software companies. Systems such as the Firefox internet browser and the Linux operating system were developed in this way. This way of working can draft, in advance, the necessary legislation to effect political change. If programmers can work in this way, lawyers can too. We can have "open source legislation". Draft legislation for voting reform and for English devolution will be ready to go. Vague and ill thought out policies will not cut it on an internet site open to all sides of the debate. Policies and ideas will be available for adoption by any of the parties. No party should be too proud to adopt a well thought out and popular policy. This part of the site could be called *The Policy Workshop*.

A new type of political organisation

CTG will not be a political party, but it will have many similar features. It will have policies in each area, pulled together by a coherent philosophy. It will have media friendly champions for each policy. It will have authoritative spokespeople for each area of government. These spokespeople will be like a "shadow cabinet" - media-friendly experts in their areas. They will critique the policies of Government and opposition and seek to provide informed comment and advice. This shadow cabinet of experts will give informed comment on hastily formed or ill-considered policies – from whichever party. These will be people who do not want to become full time politicians, do not want to actively align themselves with existing parties, but who do have something to say. They would no doubt acquit themselves very well on Question Time.

Pressure groups are not new or exciting. But what is new and exciting is a broadly-based multi-issue pressure group that has all the attributes of a political party, without being one. A political philosophy, a policy manifesto, spokespeople, a membership, influence, but no MPs. An organisation like this will be attractive to people that are passionate about politics but can't find a political party that matches their values. They can join an organisation which has political influence, and they can input into discussions over policy. They can choose to support the promotion of those policies and positions with which they agree.

Building a membership

Through policy promotion, CTG will seek to build a database of policy supporters. The whole range of social media, search engine advertising and PR tools will be used to encourage policy supporters to register. Adverts, mostly internet based, will focus on a range of popular policies and be hard-hitting and highly targeted. This process will initially be funded by the founders of CTG, but as policy supporters build, they will be offered the opportunity to fund more advertising for the policies that they support. This will allow CTG's policy campaigning to be unique, in that it will happen all the time, funded by passionate policy supporters. This will differentiate it from traditional political parties that usually only advertise at elections.

The key membership information collected will be internet contact details and postcode. This will determine in which constituency each policy supporter lives. Policy supporters will then be organised into constituency groupings. Each time a policy supporter registers to support a policy, they will be shown how many people in the same constituency have also registered to support this policy, and how many people in total. This will demonstrate the potential power of the lobby group and encourage passionate policy supporters, (e.g. for the right to die) to encourage other supporters to also register.

Membership standards

On-line discussion forums can attract people who conduct debate in an aggressive way, sometimes demonstrating extreme views. CTG will not allow that. It will publish clear values and expected standards of on-line behaviour. Full members will need to register and provide identity information. They will then be able to contribute to discussion groups. Members will be expected to identify members that do not comply with the online behaviour standards expected. These will be excluded. Members that contribute particularly informed and helpful policy ideas and feedback will be accredited by other members. Members will obtain escalating levels of recognised expertise, based on the quality of their contributions. This will be similar to the accreditation system applied to Trip Advisor reviewers.

Lobbying for change

Each political party, in each constituency, will get a regular email outlining the size of the lobby in their constituency for each of CTG's policies. National parties will be sent an email with numbers for the whole country. Political parties will be most interested in the size of the lobbies in marginal constituencies. This lobbying activity will effectively replicate the process of petitioning that was so important in generating pressure for change in nineteenth century England. The important activity of the Chartist Movement, which arose following disappointment at the limited scope of the 1832 Great Reform Act, is discussed in Chapter nine of this book. Modern Chartism has the potential to be far more effective, both through targeting MPs and their parties, and because the majority of those that have signed up to these lobby groups will have a vote, whereas most Chartists did not.

In summary, policies will be worked up by experts and enthusiasts in the policy workshop. They will be as close as possible to fully formed legislation that can be adopted off the shelf. Members of CTG will decide which polices they want to support. This will create lobby groups for these policies. Members can also choose to help grow these lobby groups by helping to fund internet advertising for the policies they support. Having outlined a philosophy, policies, recruited respected media spokespeople, and started to attract registered supporters – CTG will start to look like a potential political party. Existing political parties will become uncomfortable. CTG will have disrupted them. They will feel pressure to change, to adopt CTG policies, and to be more explicit about their own proposed policies. We want each of them to adopt as many CTG policies and ways of working as possible.

Making voting recommendations

The greatest power of an organisation like CTG comes from the potential to make a voting recommendation to their membership. This is similar to the power held by newspapers. These will usually make voting recommendations to their readerships. The Sun famously ran the headline "It's the Sun wot won it" in 1992, after their recommendation for the Conservatives helped them win the election in that year. Come election time, CTG could make a tailored voting recommendation to each member. A recommendation that would take account of the individual's declared mix of policy preferences. CTG could apply a constituency by constituency tactical voting strategy to maximise the chances of policy-friendly parties and candidates.

Moving from promoting policies to promoting individual politicians and parties that support these policies would change the nature of the organisation. It would need to register with the Electoral Commission. Under their current election expenses rules, during an election period, it would be limited to a promotional budget of a mere £31,980. That in itself need not be a problem because emailing a trusted recommendation to an existing membership would cost very little. But the election spending rules can be back-dated - to begin up to a year before an election takes place. This can bring in innocent policy advertising taking place before it is known that an election is to be held. That currently presents a barrier to a CTG type organisation engaging in voting recommendation activity. Election spending rules, and the wider remit of the Electoral Commission, are discussed in more detail at the end of this chapter.

Building a policy marketing system

During the EU referendum the power of digital targeting was used to reach voters with messages that they would react to positively. These techniques were criticised at the time, but then adopted enthusiastically by the major parties during the 2017 general election. Codes of practice for this activity are gradually emerging and will need to be at the heart of any modern system designed specifically for this purpose.

Designing and then building such a machine, using all the modern communication and analysis tools available, will need significant funding, but will be a most exciting undertaking for those involved. Important features will include a common brand and brand style which will be used for all policy advertising and PR. There will also need to be an engaging smartphone application. Anti-fraud controls will be vital to ensure that members are genuine – for example by checking for multiple applications from the same IP address. Full GDPR compliance of the database will be required as will state of the art data security.

Policy advertising on the internet will be highly targeted using search engine optimisation and pay-per-click - with a call to action, that action being to sign up. There will be integrated daytime TV, newspaper and billboard advertising – with spending focused on marginal constituencies to increase policy leverage with the candidates and parties within those constituencies. There will be an active social media presence, with a focus on obtaining celebrity endorsement - and on affinity marketing. For example, child friendly policies will be advertised on Mumsnet. There will also be an active and deep website – using friendly video messages at the front end, and with tailored web pages for each constituency. Traditional PR will also be important, producing regular press releases focused on individual policies. Regular bespoke email newsletters will be produced for members and supporters – focused on their declared policy interests. Policy experts will be made available for media comment.

Comparing political parties and candidates

The turmoil around the Brexit vote has brought home to people the importance of using their vote wisely. Their choice of political party is vital, but so too is their choice of MP. As MPs have come out from beneath the cover of their party, Brexiteers have been shocked to find that they have voted for staunch Remainers, and Remainers have been shocked to discover that they have voted for uncompromising Leavers. They will not want to make that mistake again.

In a world where there is more choice and more information, how should people make these important personal decisions? Comparison websites such as Compare the Market and Money Supermarket show how this process might develop in the political marketplace. Developments like this are already taking place. Samuel Fishwick, in the London Evening Standard examines how technology is being used to help make "tactical voting smarter". In particular, he looks at how the internet and apps were used to help people make choices in the 2017 election. An app called Tactical 2017 helped those that wanted to vote strategically to unseat the Conservatives. Spokesperson Becky Snowden said, "With access to this information in our phones, we literally have the power to bring about change in our hands." Meanwhile, Voting Counts is a website set up by student Rachel Farringdon. At the 2017 election this site extracted content from a variety of sources, collating, rewriting, and simplifying it, free of bias. "We try to help young adults compare the main party policies, enabling them to make their own decisions uninfluenced by friends and family." The Daily Election app gamifies the political experience asking topical political questions, the answers to which will determine whether you will end up as Prime Minister or Pleb. There is even a political version of Tinder, which allows you to swipe "yes" or "no" to political ideas.

These various consumer sites are just the beginning. At the next election there will be a proliferation of political sites like these, helping people to make choices. We need to make sure that they have adequate and correct information to use.

Regulation of political comparison sites

Before big buying decisions most people now use the internet to research their choices. It makes sense to provide the electorate with a user-friendly site to help them find out where parties and candidates stand on the issues they care about before they vote for them. At election time, this site will force politicians and parties to be explicit about their views and policy proposals, providing short Twitter style responses to a number of questions. These can then be compared.

Mysociety.org with its website Theyworkforyou.com has done a fantastic job in setting up a framework to report back factually and authoritatively on the work and opinions of MP's in office. There is a gap in the market that a trusted and independent organisation, such as Mysociety, could possibly fill. We need an independent and trusted organisation to help the electorate compare the policies of parties, and the opinions of candidates, in an unbiased and a structured manner - before an election. This site would need strong independent governance. Some parties and candidates might not want to play ball. But the electorate will make their own minds up on parties or candidates that refuse to tell us what they think about the issues we care about.

Another way to ensure adequate and accurate information will be to bring in a requirement for parties and candidates to provide it. This could be built into the new election rules set out in Chapter 2. The Electoral Commission would be the obvious body to collect and make this information available. They will determine the format of the policy information to be provided by parties and candidates before an election. This information will be fed into the Electoral Commission website by candidates and parties - and then made publicly available to voters and to comparison organisations.

The need for an authorised site is clear. Authorised information can then be used by both pressure-group sites and consumer comparison sites. Pressure group sites will use the information to give those that have registered with them a recommendation for the candidate and party in their constituency that is most likely to further their policy choices. Comparison sites will use this information to allow voters to make more informed decisions. These types of organisation should need to register with the Electoral Commission. The Commission will need to consider appropriate regulation to ensure accuracy and a lack of bias in their recommendation algorithms. However, that regulation should not be so restrictive that it suppresses the formation of these types of organisations. Comparison sites will represent a good way to make it easier for people to engage with the political process - and to make more informed decisions.

Establishing political comparison sites for consumers

If authorised responses to questions are not available, comparison organisations will do this work themselves. They will do this by taking extracts from manifestos and charting what is said by each party and candidate during a campaign. That is what CTG will do. This will demonstrate where parties and candidates stand on its policy agenda. CTG will establish two separately branded comparison websites, set up like insurance price comparison websites, or dating sites. At an election people will score each party and candidate's views on the issues they care about. At the end, the sites will score each of the political parties and local candidates against that person's own views and preferences and produce a match. People will be matched with the candidate and party that most closely match to their beliefs and policy preferences.

These consumer sites will put pressure on candidates and parties. They will fund themselves through discrete web-based advertising from political candidates, parties, and registered policy pressure groups. The advertising spending of these organisations during an election period is controlled under the election spending rules. These consumer sites will get some of this compliant spending, rather than it all going to Facebook or Google. The sites will develop a GDPR compliant user database.

The first CTG comparison website will be Compare-The-Party.uk. People will fill out a template listing the issues that they most care about. The site will then return each party's views on these issues – Twitter style - with a limited number of words to aid comparison. The answers will be linked to their manifestos. There will also be the opportunity for each party leader to generate a short video explaining why people should vote for their party. The second comparison website will be Compare-The-Candidate.uk. Voters will use this site to make comparisons between candidates that put themselves up for election in their own constituency. There will be a structured set of questions for candidates to answer which will probe candidates' views on social as well as policy issues. The site will also hold videos from each candidate - outlining why voters should choose them.

Can we choose how to vote in the same way as we buy car insurance? Yes, we can. If we take the dating site analogy, many people now choose their life partner in this way. People will want to use the same approach to choose their MP, and their political parties. This process will be vastly preferable to using the mixed set of dubious claims and edited policy lists from parties and candidates that land through our letter boxes prior to election day. It is almost impossible to choose candidates and parties based on the type of material they send us. Much of this material Mr Trump would call "Fake News". We should make our comparisons on a more logical and structured basis. Make candidates and parties answer the questions we want to ask, rather than the ones they want to be asked, and compare their answers on the same basis.

Imagine how powerful for democracy it would be if comparison sites become the places to go to before you decide how to vote. Imagine how incumbent MPs and incumbent political parties would hate them – having to give concise and clear answers to direct questions for a change. Imagine how this could disrupt politics.

The Electoral Commission

The Electoral Commission is the independent body which oversees elections and regulates political finance in the UK. It works to promote public confidence in the democratic process and ensure its integrity. The Commission's mandate was set out in the Political Parties, Elections and Referendums Act 2000 (PPERA), and ranges from the regulation of political donations and expenditure by political and third parties through to promoting greater participation in the electoral process. It seems as though the Electoral Commission has been around forever, but they are a recent development in the context of British political history. Before 2001 political donations were secret, parties did not have to say who was funding them, and there were no spending limits during election campaigns.

The Electoral Commission is a force for good, and its website is an excellent source of information. It is the obvious organisation to control the enhanced procedures for parties during elections outlined in Chapter 2. It should be an ally for the proposals in this book. Proposals that are designed to strengthen peoples' control over political parties and to improve political decision making and choice. But any fundamental review of the democratic processes we operate will also need to look at whether the rules that the Electoral Commission enforces are hampering the necessary evolution of the system.

Business knows that overly complex and burdensome regulation is always to the advantage of existing companies, and to the disadvantage of start-up challenger competitors. This seems to have happened in the political marketplace. Are Electoral Commission rules overly protecting existing parties and organisations and inhibiting the development of new ones? At first sight the answer to that question is no. The Electoral Commission website shows that we have 380 political parties registered, many of them recently. But a closer examination of the election expenses rules shows how these work in favour of existing national parties.

A registered political party is allowed to spend £30,000 for each constituency that it contests. A party fighting 650 seats could spend £19.5 million across the UK. Locally, a candidate can only spend £8,700 plus six pence or nine pence per registered parliamentary voter in the constituency, depending on the type of constituency. These rules give a huge advantage to large existing parties. This is particularly so since evidence suggests that national budgets are not spent evenly but are focused on marginal seats. Safe seats need little attention. The Commission is aware of this trend and how social media targeting magnifies it.

All parties spent widely on Google and Facebook advertising in the last election, with the Conservatives spending over £2m on Facebook, and the parties together spending over half a million pounds on Google. These payments went to Facebook Ireland and Google Ireland by the way – so I am not sure quite how feeding these foreign based organisations with so much money can be good for our democracy, but that is another point. The main point is that living in a safe seat, I didn't see a single political advert, so somebody else must be getting my share.

There are two potential changes that will help. The first is a tiered rule for the amount available for election expenses. For example, a party registering to fight five constituencies will get an election expense allocation of £100,000 per constituency. The next twenty constituencies fought will attract an allocation of £75,000 per constituency, and the next hundred £50,000. Beyond that, parties will get an allowance of £20,000 per extra constituency. This change will help new parties to establish themselves and help smaller parties to compete for marginal constituencies on a more level playing field. The second change will be a much tighter and better-defined rule in respect of the period to which the election expenses rules apply. The demonstrable ability of Governments to get around the fixed term election rules, and to call a snap election, means that campaigning organisations and new political organisations establishing themselves can get innocently caught by them. These rules should only apply once an election has been announced.

Finally, the Commission's website is so impressive that it is clear that it can only be one step away from people being able to use it to register their vote. That step is the introduction of a robust national identity scheme, as discussed and recommended later in this book.

4

THE NEW POLITICS

The first few years of the twenty-first century, culminating in the Brexit and Trump votes, will come to be seen as the moment when the politics of culture and identity rose to challenge the politics of left and right.

David Goodhart, The Road to Somewhere

New ways of thinking, new allegiances and new technology are beginning to break down traditional political groupings and traditional ways of doing things. These changes are examined here and will be a challenge for traditional party structures. As the Dominic Cummings character said in Brexit: the uncivil war, "There is a new politics in town – one that you cannot control".

Representative democracy

During the elevator pitch process, one concern expressed was that this proposal would clash with Britain's system of representative democracy. We elect politicians who use their knowledge and intellect to decide what is best for us. The principle was explained by Walter Bagehot (pronounced like "gadget") who studied mathematics at UCL and went on to marry the daughter of the owner of The Economist magazine. He was its editor for 17 years and The Economist continues to run a column in his name. Bagehot wrote about representative democracy in his 1867 book, The English Constitution, with a second edition in 1872, after the second Reform Act of 1867. This Act enfranchised part of the urban male working class for the first time so that they could vote. The book is still described as the definitive text on the British political system.

Bagehot believed that MPs are paid to be representatives, not delegates. "They should obey their own judgement over the rolling opinions of their constituents." This builds upon the views of Edmund Burke, as expressed in his speech to the Electors of Bristol in 1774, where he famously notes that "Your representative owes you, not his industry only, but his judgement: and he betrays instead of serving you, if he sacrifices it to your opinion". Burke was arguing against MPs taking authoritative instructions from their electorate. Professor Jonathan Clarke notes an example of this type of MP, Andrew Marvell, MP for Hull in 1659-78. He was paid by his constituents and regularly reported back to them. Clarke observes that in comparison to Marvell's straight forward approach, Burke's high-sounding doctrine did not prove popular with his own constituents. They threw him out for favouring Irish commercial interests over their own.

The CTG lobby system will not weaken representative democracy. The principle of an informed voter lobby is nothing new, it will just be made to operate more effectively. In some circumstances it will strengthen the power of individual MPs against their parties. The Economist notes that a vote that angers local constituents will no longer go unnoticed. The increased willingness to defy the party whips is partly due to MPs fear of their constituents. Websites such as Theyworkforyou.com make it possible to find out an MP's voting record in a few clicks, rather than by wading through Hansard.

At the core of both Bagehot's and Burke's views on representative democracy was a belief that most voters do not have the capacity to make informed decisions for themselves. Bagehot wrote that MP's were voted in by the "ignorant classes" to make decisions on their behalf. Parliament and the House of Lords were "dignified institutions", whose pomp and ceremony were there to impress. Parliament was supported by "efficient institutions", staffed by the elite. But many things have changed since 1867. The dignified institutions of British Government are no longer so dignified. Most people would not call our government institutions efficient. But the biggest change is in attitudes. People no longer have unquestioning respect or belief in authority. We are no longer content to know our place.

The representative democracy system of 1867 was operating at a time when the "ruling class" was infinitely better informed and educated than voters. That is no longer the case. Education, TV and the media have beaten back ignorance. The internet gives us instant access to information. Easily accessed media of all kinds discuss and analyse political issues 24/7. People no longer want to elect someone that knows what is best for them. They know that themselves. They want to elect someone whose values and outlook on life align with their own. They want to elect a party whose policies they believe in. These may be two different things. This is why it is unsatisfactory that our current system fuses these two things into one vote. That means that we do not get the best people into parliament, and we do not get parties to adopt the best policies. The other problem is that whereas in 1867 it might have been possible to become elected as an MP under your own steam, and then choose which policies and party to support, today that is virtually impossible. If you do not have a political party behind you, you are most unlikely to get elected. This gives huge power to those that control political parties. It also gives a huge disincentive for MPs to obey their own judgements over their party's.

Many things have changed since Bagehot's day, but the basic structure of how our democracy works has not changed. British reverence for tradition has held back the evolution of our democratic institutions. Structures and processes are creaking everywhere. Parliament and our Civil Service no longer attract our best people. Our MPs are trapped in a system where their political parties are calling the shots. Neither they nor their constituents can do much about it. Or can they? The previous two chapters outline changes designed to strengthen our democracy. Changes that will put legally binding structure and timetables behind how political parties formulate manifestos and policies. Structures that will stop them from going "off-piste" once in power. And key to change, the introduction of a more representative voting system that will allow new parties and ideas to develop.

Individual candidate support for a charter of political reform, either before or after being elected, would be true to representative democracy, true to Burke's requirement of MPs that they obey their own judgement. This judgement would be backed by a powerful lobby of charter supporting voters in their constituency.

Will the major parties allow their MPs and candidates to have independent views on issues so important to their continued control of power? Probably not, but in that instance individual conscience and representative democracy will come into conflict with party loyalty. If ever we are ripe for a rebellion, a rebellion of MPs against their parties, it is now. MPs must put aside their political allegiances to work together to improve the rules by which their parties play this game.

Bagehot wrote his book at a time when the second Reform Act brought in fundamental change to the political system which dramatically extended the right to vote. The public was able to pressure politicians to implement this important change. We need just such pressure now, to enable a new Reform Act. For MPs that are unhappy with the directions of their parties, unhappy about how decisions are made, there should be no need to leave those parties. All it will take is courage and faith. Courage to stand up for electoral reform, while staying within their parties. Faith in democracy. Faith in the British people to use an improved system of democracy to produce better political parties and better government.

Populism

When formulating my plans, it dawned on me that because I want a method to lobby for popular policies, I must be a "populist". What's wrong with being popular I thought. But this is a derogatory term, used most often by those in power to put-down people who disagree with them. Wikipedia defines a populist as an adherent to a political party seeking to represent the interests of ordinary people. Populists attempt to unite the "common person" against "corrupt dominant elites". That sounds pretty cool to me.

Populists have acquired their bad reputation because populist politicians can pursue popular policies before an election. Once in power, they quietly drop them, becoming part of the corrupt dominant elite themselves. That is one of the reasons that people are so interested to see whether Donald Trump does follow through on the populist policies he espoused during his election campaign. Another problem with populists is that they tend to be led by strong charismatic leaders. Once in power these leaders can start to make it difficult to remove them. They clamp down on critical elements of the media. They can also change the political rules to keep themselves in power. Aristotle warned against populists. "Sometimes, by using fraud people manage at first to obtain the consent of the population for a change in the constitution: but later they keep control of affairs in the face of general dissent." Populists are usually characterised as right-wing, but they can equally come to power through espousing radically socialist agendas, or, indeed, environmental ones. We are also beginning to see the emergence of pro-European populist parties in the UK, as evidenced by the Liberal Democrats' "Bollocks to Brexit" campaign in the recent European elections.

Despite these dangers of populism, in any battle between the common people and the dominant elite, I'm with the common people. In Star Wars, I'm going to be one of the rebels. But I recognise that this cause is open to abuse by charlatans and autocrats. That is why we must strengthen the checks and balances in our system.

Identity politics

Identity politics are political positions based on the interests and perspectives of social groups with which people identify. Examples include age, religion, social class, culture, disability, education, ethnicity, language, nationality, sex, gender identity, generation, occupation, and sexual orientation. Professor Weale discusses identity politics in his book, The Will of The People. "The stable, boring politics of two-party competition for the centre voter, side-lining some issues, has been broken apart through the creation of new forces that focus on the politics of race, gender, the environment and social morality. In turn, mobilisation around these issues has caused a counter-revolution led by nationalist and morally conservative forces."

Identity politics was previously catered for by mainstream political parties in their appeals to class. The working class would have been largely Labour; the managerial class largely Conservative. But we now have a much more complicated tapestry of identities and allegiances. This development has been helped by social media and academics. Identity politics is particularly strong in our universities. The phrase "woke" is used to explain the process by which people "wake up" to become aware of their own identity, and the identity of others. This process can bring with it a realisation or a belief that certain parts of the identity spectrum have been oppressed by other parts of it. In some instances, this creates anger and an intolerance of traditional or alternative views. Jenny McCartney explains this, "Where progressive movements of the past emphasised shared values and goals, identity politics divides people into categories – mainly according to gender, race and sexuality – and constructs a hierarchy based on the perceived intensity of oppression endured by each group."

Identity politics can bring with it a lack of acceptance of people's rights to hold alternative views. This can result in a refusal to hear or engage with these views. This can encompass the concept on "non-platforming", where there is an attempt to stop people with alternative views from having a public platform to express and discuss these views. There can also be a belief that historical characters should be judged against the values of our time, as opposed to the values of the time in which they lived. Many people see identity politics as the new extremism. They feel oppressed by political correctness. There are troubling aspects to attempts to impose a value set on others that do not feel that way. These developments have been accompanied by a tightening up of the boundaries of the right to free speech. But despite these concerns, there is no doubt that strong feelings of identity will continue to shape our politics, even though to many people a focus on identity issues - and on "me", will seem like a luxury while there are people sleeping on the streets, people without enough to eat, young people being stabbed.

"Somewheres" and "Anywheres"

David Goodhart's book, The Road to Somewhere, uses identity politics to explain some of the tribalism around Brexit. He describes people who do not align themselves with any one country, considering themselves to be citizens of the world. These "People from Anywhere" are usually urban dwelling, better educated, and highly mobile. They interact with similar people in other countries and will feel at home anywhere. They see responsibilities as global and that we have obligations to all human beings, not just those that live in our country.

People from Anywhere are not a modern phenomenon. These

are possibly the people that Aristotle was referring to in his book, Politics. "He who is without a city, by reason of his own nature, and not of some accident, is either a poor sort of being, or a being higher than man: he is like the man of whom Homer wrote in denunciation: Clanless and lawless and heartless is he." Goodhart compares these people to "People from Somewhere". These people are patriotic and valuing of local community. They do not believe that we have the same obligations to people everywhere as we have to our own citizens. They believe that we should focus our resources on solving the problems that we have in our own communities.

The case for Anywheres is given by the Economist in their review of Goodhart's book. "Why should national or racial attachments take priority over common humanity? Why should accommodating those who have such attachments justify excluding poor foreigners from economic opportunity? Just why is it "common sense" that national citizens should be ahead of non-citizens in the queue for public goods?" But for those that do believe that national citizens should be ahead of the queue, and I am one of these, then this shows what an important political theme this is. Voters are beginning to look carefully at where their party and MP stands on Somewhere versus Anywhere issues.

Open and closed

Another way of dividing people into political categories is the division between Open and Closed, rather than Left and Right. Openness is the support for both economic openness (welcoming immigration and free trade) and cultural openness (embracing ethnic and sexual minorities). Closedness means the opposite.

London is an Open city. Those that live there see heart-warming things every day. School kids from every European nation - but all the same in their awkward geekiness and lack of confidence. Mixed-race young couples, very much in love. Same-sex couples, hand in hand. Two people chatting, one in English, the other responding in French. A vibrant and exciting city, welcoming, confident, tolerant, and at peace with itself. But to retain this harmony we need control of our borders. Be open to those we invite, rather than those that just decide to come here. The Economist notes that having a strong border can make people more open, by giving them a sense that they can manage openness. "Historically, most of the world's greatest centres of commerce have been walled cities."

An important aspect of Openness is for openness from those that live here. This will include a willingness to provide identity and personal data. As David Goodhart notes: "We need to return to the debate about ID cards and a population register. Many people who voted for Brexit have an uneasy sense that the authorities do not know how many people are here or where they are. And they are right." We need to know more about the people living here to help us to protect our borders, and so that we can care for and protect those legitimately within them.

The GAL – TAN spectrum

In European politics, in addition to the old left-right spectrum, there is now the GAL–TAN spectrum. That is Green, Alternative and Libertarian versus Traditional, Authoritarian and Nationalist. Professor Weale helps frame some of these choices. "Some people want an open and liberal society even at the cost of some social disorder, whereas others want a stable and conformist society even at the cost of intolerance. Some people are prepared to allow for greater economic inequality in order to promote entrepreneurship, whereas others favour greater equality even if there is less wealth to spread around." I see myself on the Green, Alternative and Liberal side of the equation. That surprised me, since I do not empathise with the current political parties that occupy this space. Although their values are good, many of their policies are not. There is space here. Space for a political party that respects GAL values, while choosing different policies. In particular, policies that respect free enterprise, equality, and the need for economic as well as environmental responsibility.

Internationalists and Nationalists

Another political dividing line, similar to Anywheres and Somewheres, is Internationalists, who expect us to care for all people equally and Nationalists, who don't accept that people who are not our citizens should enjoy the same rights and privileges as those that are. Some Internationalists believe that we should allow open borders. The Economist argues this case based upon the increase in the income and well-being of the migrants that come here. The alternative view is put by the economist Roger Bootle: "the idea that there is no divergence between the private self-interest of an immigrant coming here, and the social interest of the British people in admitting that immigrant, is just ridiculous." Bootle's point was made well by an Italian citizen in the south, while observing her town swamped by poor and helpless migrants. "We are helping everybody, but nobody is helping us." Similar feelings of abandonment are at work in other countries, and in some cases are driving people towards extremist politics. Despite this, the view that global welfare is paramount to national welfare still exists in large parts of our political establishment.

Undemocratic liberalism

To protect the 49% from the potential tyranny of the 51%, we have a legal system of individual rights and checks and balances. In the last decade this system has grown to become very extensive and more restrictive. Many issues are now removed from national democratic choice thanks to developments like independent central banks and human rights laws. The courts have shaped how rules and laws are interpreted and operated – sometimes taking them beyond what was envisaged when they were originally framed. Some argue that this legal framework is too liberal and restrictive, and that we now have a system of intrenched undemocratic liberalism. Democrats argue that we need to retain a democratic power to sweep some of this away. That is one of the concerns of liberals in relation to the UK's potential exit from the EU. Our membership of the EU stops this from happening. Others argue that our courts are to blame. We should reduce the width that our own courts have applied to laws on individual rights. These laws are there to protect us, but their use seems to be protecting those that don't deserve that protection or are twisting them to gain an advantage. This brings important and sensible laws into disrepute.

Illiberal democracy

The attraction of populism to voters is a global phenomenon. It is a particular worry for the EU. In many European countries democracy is a relatively recent development. They do not have the deep system of checks and balances we find here. In Europe, the election of fascists and dictators did not happen that long ago. Hitler was voted into power. This is one of the reasons that the EU is so keen on its rules-based system.

Within the EU we have countries trending towards authoritarianism. Viktor Orban, Hungary's Prime Minister, is an enthusiastic proponent of "illiberal democracy". He set out the case for illiberal democracy in his speech at Baile Tusnad in 2014. Orban believes that a democracy does not necessarily need to be liberal. That "societies founded on the principle of the liberal way to organise a state will not be able to sustain their world competitiveness in the following years." He has been vilified for his views on migration, and for systematically weakening institutions that provide oversight and transparency, such as the media. But his government remains popular with Hungarian voters.

Orban explores the practical impact of having too great an emphasis on individual legal freedoms. Individual rights are only valued when they can be protected, but "the weak are not able to take on the strong when the strong do something that impacts on the weak's freedom." He has become a champion of those that see their right to hold illiberal views and to support illiberal parties being gradually eroded.

The People Vs. Democracy

Yascha Mounk's book, of this title, discusses the growing battle between illiberal democracy, or democracy without rights on the one hand, and undemocratic liberalism, or rights without democracy, on the other. "The popular will is increasingly coming into contact with individual rights. Liberal elites are willing to exclude the people from important decisions, most notably about immigration in the case of the EU, in the name of rights. Meanwhile populists are willing to dispense with constitutional niceties in the name of the people." Mounk is concerned that people are increasingly not valuing or defending their democratic freedoms and are seduced by autocratic leaders. These leaders, once voted in, might then take those democratic freedoms away. He has some compelling statistics to back up this concern. He worries that we might be on the verge of a new "populist age" that could last for 20 to 30 years.

In Mounk's TED lecture, he cites a lack of economic progress as the main reason that people are turning away from democracy. I suspect that equally important driving forces are a lack of perceived power to effect change, and a lack of credible and distinctive political choices. Increasing income and wealth inequality, both at an individual and regional level, will also be having an impact.

The non-liberal changes that Mounk fears will be introduced without a mandate by populist parties are mirrored by many of the internationalist and liberal changes that have been introduced without a clear mandate by liberal parties. Both extremes need better control. A more extensive rules-based system for how political parties operate is needed. A more explicit process for obtaining democratic mandates for the changes that political parties want to make. More checks and balances on how they wield power. Better political choices. A fairer and more representative voting system. More devolution of power. These are the things that will protect our democracy.

E-democracy

Iceland's Pirate Party and Italy's Five Star movement (founded by the comedian Beppe Grillo) use the internet to engage their membership in policy making directly. The internet allows direct and immediate contact with more citizens than ever before. The Five Star movement sees e-democracy, or "direct democracy", as an evolution of the principles of representative democracy. "Iceland's Pirate Party are not here to gain power - they are here to distribute power." They were founded in November 2012. Adoption of a policy hinges on the ability to root it firmly in the core policies of the party. It must also receive sufficient support in the Pirate Party's online voting system, which is the primary method through which Pirates settle disputes and reach consensus on policies. The Pirate website explains that all party work depends on the participation of individuals. Discussions are spread over in-house meetings, social media and various online groups. A great deal of dialogue takes place on Facebook pages, but there are also more focused web discussions where Icelandic Pirates debate, interact and reach consensus on a variety of topics. In the words of Gilbert and Sullivan, "it would be a glorious thing, to be a pirate king". This does look like a good idea, a way forward for democracy. Early adopters, like Italy's Five Star Movement, are likely to have radical agendas, but that does not take away from the legitimacy of their methods. There is much to admire.

The first-past-the-post system in the UK is currently a barrier to the development of Pirate-like parties here. But many of their ideas and ways of working can be adopted to mobilise and involve people in an attempt to help change this system.

Conclusion

Walter Bagehot observed that we were essentially a moderate country. This is still true today. We do not have an appetite for illiberal democracy. But we also do not have an appetite for the extremes of undemocratic liberalism. Radically "progressive" policies, for example on immigration and wealth redistribution, and yes, on extreme CO_2 reduction targets too, should not be pursued without a clear and explicit mandate. The refusal to countenance dissent or to hear alternative viewpoints is dangerous. These things can produce a reaction. Democracies have demonstrated that voters can be seduced by the attractions of authoritarian illiberal democracy.

Our democracy puts itself at risk when it restricts its ability to change, or when it puts itself at the mercy of unaccountable institutions. Our democracy puts itself at risk when in the face of obvious injustice or things that are not working, our politicians put their hands-up and say, "There's nothing we can do about this." A large part of the energy that drove the Brexit vote was a desire to return to empowered, accountable and democratic self-government. But most of us would not want to live in Viktor Orban's Hungary. We want self-government, but not an authoritarian government. We need protections from those that would take our freedoms away.

5

POLITICAL VALUES

The moral principles and beliefs or accepted standards of a person or social group.
One's judgement of what is important in life.

Definition of 'values', Oxford English Dictionary

This chapter explores political values. These are key to defining each political party. They express the type of country that each party wants to build, their aspirations for the people within it, and their priorities for policy formation. In previous centuries political values largely sprung from the predominant national religion. In the western world, this has been Christianity. As such, many values were implicit and "taken as read". We did not need to write them down. Today's world is more complicated, not just because of the multiplicity of religions, but because of the increase in the number of powerful nations that do not share our values.

Modern political unions, like CTG, will be values based. Their policies and positions will flow from their values, which will be clearly articulated. In this way they can reject policy ideas that are not consistent with their values. They can also terminate the membership of people whose behaviour and opinions are out of step with their values. The values explored in this chapter are essentially personal. With more political choice, each of us will benefit from deciding what we believe in, and then comparing this against the political choices that are available. We cannot rely on past choices. Some of those parties that we used to support have changed and moved away from us. Sometimes, we will have changed and moved away from them. Each reader will find important omissions, and also statements with which they disagree. That is the nature of politics. This section is here to challenge and to prompt.

Patriotism

The dictionary defines patriotism as the feeling of loving your country more than any others and being proud of it. Some parts of our society see patriotism as dangerous and look down on people for whom this is important. Most of us are in the other camp. We think that it is important that we should love our country. But which country is that? I feel mostly associated with England, but I am also British. When I must choose my nationality from drop-down menus on travel sites, I am from The United Kingdom. What is that? Nobody calls themselves a United Kingdomer. It turns out that the United Kingdom is Great Britain with Northern Ireland thrown in. Great Britain is also a curious term. British people are usually self-effacing. When did we start calling ourselves "Great"? Apparently, it was not us that first started calling ourselves Great, it was the French. The term Great Britain served to distinguish the large island of Britain from the French region of Brittany (in French Grande-Bretagne and Bretagne respectively). Maybe not so great then.

We have a unifying monarch, but nobody calls her the Queen of the UK. She is usually referred to as the Queen of England. We have a British Parliament, but we don't have an English parliament. Scotland, Wales and Ireland have their own national anthems, but the English don't. When England play rugby against one of the other home nations, the English sing the British national anthem, God Save the Queen, as their own. That's always a bit awkward. If we are patriotic, which flag should we fly, the Union Flag or the cross of St George? It's probably best to fly both unless you want to make a statement. And why do all those other countries still have a Union Flag on their own national flags? What's the whole Commonwealth thing about? The old are proud of it, the young, somewhat bemused by it.

If you are looking to choose a political party, their views on patriotism will be important. This will form the cornerstone on which they will build and execute their policies. What makes them proud about our country? Can they express this in words? Here is my attempt.

Being English is possessing a quiet knowledge that you are part of the greatest country there has ever been. A diverse nation of creative, tolerant, friendly and humorous people. The home of the industrial revolution. The inheritor of a long and proud history of independence, and of fighting for what is right. A people united by a common language, a common outlook on life, and thousands of years of culture. A beautiful island of green fields, windswept beaches, bluebells, roses, warm summer evenings and crisp frosty mornings. A fertile country teeming with wildlife. A country of castles, manor houses, rivers and canals, horses, pubs, cricket, village fetes and real ale.

I also feel British. I am equally proud of that, although I don't have the same love for Britain as I do for England. Being British is more values-based. It is how we behave and present ourselves to the world. The British Club is not exclusive. It is a set of values, not an accident of birth. Anyone should be able to call themselves British if they sign up to the values. We see people from all parts of the world happy to associate with, and wear, the British flag. Other countries still incorporate the British Union Flag in their own national flags. It means something. When I think of Britain, I see a way of organising ourselves. Setting aside national interests in the pursuit of a larger common aim. I see national pride and diversity welcomed and celebrated. I see the development of parliamentary democracy, the rule of law, and the rights of the individual against the state. I see an outward looking world view. Friendly relationships with like-minded countries. I see international influence and respect. I think of British institutions like the BBC, the NHS, and our Armed Forces. I see the development of a welfare system that looks after those in need. I am incredibly proud to be British.

I am proud to be English and British, but I also feel European. I like rubbing shoulders with people from Italy, France, Spain, Poland, and Germany, and feeling that we are part of the same European family. I feel connected with a shared European heritage and a common view on life. But despite our shared geography and history, although I am still going to be European, I am not going to be part of the EU for much longer. Like all divorces, this makes me sad. There is much to like about the EU. I like the EU's funky blue flag. I like having an EU passport. I enjoy border-free travel in Europe. I like the feeling of being part of something that is big enough to stand up to countries like the USA, China and Russia. I like a forum for our leaders to get together and talk about big issues. I am sad about losing these things. I hope that in our new relationship with the EU, an accommodation can eventually be reached where many of these things will endure.

Part of patriotism is having pride in your country. Too much pride can promote arrogance and overconfidence, of which the English, in particular, can be guilty. But if we don't have pride in our country, our institutions, our towns, our families and ourselves, then we become satisfied with low standards. We expect too little. Tolerance of litter is an example of a lack of pride. Mile after mile of litter-filled verges. Not just on motorways, in towns as well. Good businesses don't tolerate shabby offices or messy working conditions. This generates a lack of pride and results in poor customer service. We need national pride, but we also need civic pride. The sort of pride that would not tolerate begging and rough sleeping on our streets. National and civic pride should make us want to sort these things out. It should make us want to elect politicians who are prepared to get down and dirty. To get in the weeds. To make things work properly. To take control and responsibility. It should make us tell our politicians that these things are just not acceptable. And it should make us get up early in the morning to write a book like this...

Democracy

One of the essences of being British is a belief in democracy. Our arguments happen in Parliament and are vocal and boisterous. They are decided by a vote – and then everyone gets on and does what has been decided, even if they did not agree with it. For those of us that believe in our democracy, the problems following the EU referendum have been painful to behold. Parliament has been instructed by the people to enact a policy that the vast majority of its members do not support. Democracy by referendum, and representative democracy, have clashed. This will play out over a number of years but has identified weaknesses in our democratic system. Our system has produced a disproportionate number of MPs that have markedly different views to their constituents. If those constituents feel let down by their representatives, then they will demand better choices at the next election, or they will abandon their faith in democracy entirely. Fixing and improving Britain's democratic processes must now be a priority.

An important part of this fixing will be more devolution. Aristotle notes, "Experience shows that it is difficult, if not indeed impossible, for a very populous city to enjoy good government. Observation tells us that none of the cities which have a reputation for being well governed are without some limit of population." Andy Burnham, Mayor of Greater Manchester, believes that devolution is the best way of making government more intelligent, as well as more accountable. It shortens the feedback loop between problems and solutions. Robert Satchwell gives the example of Denmark, which has fewer people than London, but has three elected tiers of government: local, regional, and national. Each tier has clearly defined responsibilities and the power to raise the money to finance them. Income-tax rates can vary from commune to commune.

With a more devolved system there is a greater opportunity to consult the people through internet forums, surveys, and local referendums on social and local issues. Switzerland, a country of 8.5 million people, supports direct democracy and held 10 national referendums in 2018. In the USA, referendums happen at state level. California has held 50 referendums since 1912. Ireland also holds referendums, but sensibly applies Article 46 of its constitution whereby people vote on a change only after a bill has been drafted which includes all of the details.

A modern democracy should have a written constitution. We have an opportunity to produce one for the first time. A document that people from around the world will recognise as encapsulating the essence of British democratic values and character. Something that will put meaning behind the Union Flag. Being "British" should be the gold-standard for citizenship and democracy around the world.

Sustainability

We value and celebrate diversity. But we also want balance and harmony. Open borders do not allow us to plan for the numbers of people arriving. This puts pressure on our ecosystem, on our housing, health, transport and education systems. We need to protect our environment and to ensure that our infrastructure can cope. We must be compassionate, but we must control inward migration.

An increasing population is attractive to politicians. They want Britain to have more power and a bigger voice in the world. Economists also like it. Importing workers into the population means there are more people to pay off our national debt. Businesses like it too, since it produces larger markets and access to an unending supply of cheap labour. But for those of us that don't like crowds, those of us that value quiet and solitude, those of us that have to compete with newcomers for jobs and public services, those of us that have to fight for space on pavements and roads, a higher density of population damages our quality of life. UK population has increased by seven million since the turn of the century, 82% of this increase is attributable to migration. England now stands second only to the Netherlands in European population density.

Sometimes, migration can help achieve balance and sustainability. Japan has closed borders and is not ethnically diverse. Their low birth rate has produced a severe demographic challenge. They have an increasing older population supported by a reducing number of younger people. The population is declining. Some towns are dying, their young people moving to more dynamic and mixed areas. There is cultural harmony, but there is not balance. We don't want this. Much inward migration to the UK has been of young, skilled, and economically active people. This has been positive for us. We have a youthful energy. But we do need to be able to control and plan these numbers, and to seek an eventual balance.

Regional policy within the UK can play a part. There has been too much of a focus on the South East, parts of which have become uncomfortably densely populated. We can also use our overseas development spending more intelligently. Our communities should seek to become more self-sufficient. Let's not be embarrassed by a preference to buy locally, to buy British. Not only does consuming locally produced goods help local communities, it also helps the environment by reducing transport costs and associated pollution. To many, the feel-good factor of consuming something made here increases its value for us. We are prepared to pay a bit more for something we know has been made locally. The City of Preston in Lancashire has shown the way. It has leaned upon its public institutions, such as its university and hospital, to source locally.

We can also seek sustainability and self-sufficiency in energy production. Advances in battery technology, together with cheaper and more effective solar and wind turbines, makes energy generation and self-sufficiency in communities more practical. If we combine these with investment in tidal schemes and better insulated houses, we can make good strides towards national energy self-sufficiency and a low carbon footprint.

All these good things will only be possible if we have sustainability in our national finances. We don't have that now. We have a public debt which gets bigger every year. We spend £50 billion each year on interest to service it. That is more than we spend on the police and the armed forces combined. Those politicians that expect the debt problem to be fixed by economic growth, sometime in the future, need to explain where this growth is to come from. A lot of our economic growth over the last decade has come from immigration, creating a bigger population. Is that what the public wants? Paying for public services by increasing the size of the working population by migration has been described as a "demographic and fiscal Ponzi scheme". As these new people age and draw on public services, even more migration will be needed to attract yet more working people to support them. In a densely populated country like England, this is not a viable or attractive policy for the long term.

Protecting our environment and taking sensible and sustained action to bear down on CO_2 emissions is another important element of sustainability. But a plan for CO_2 reduction needs to be developed together with a plan for our economy. Tipping points do not just occur in the natural environment, they occur in economics as well. There is a parallel between the accumulation of CO_2 in the atmosphere, and our accumulating national debt. Both, if not tackled, could have serious consequences for the futures of our young people. We need a plan for economic progress which is sustainable and non-polluting. A plan which makes us an example to the world of how to run a harmonious, sustainable and successful post-industrial society.

Freedom

It is strange how we interpret personal freedom in our country. In some areas we are incredibly liberal, in others quite unreasonably authoritarian and controlling. Our framework of checks and balances has developed alongside our prevailing religious beliefs, and in a pre-technological era. Political parties can differentiate themselves in this important area and give us some clear choices.

Generally, we are a very free country. This is one of the reasons that people want to live here. We are free to go where we like, dress how we like, eat what we want, and to live how we want. That is one of the essential essences of being British. We have also made good strides on freedom of information. The main freedom gaps we have are in public health. We have controlling and moralising medical and legal professions and a still powerful religious lobby. For example, we don't give terminally ill people the right to decide the timing of their own death. The state takes away the most important and personal decision they will ever make. Responsible and informed soft drug users are criminalised. We can do things better. Other countries are showing the way. Road use is another area which is overdue a review. Pavements are a better place for young people on bicycles than roads. And we should make our traffic lights, speed limits, and enforcement devices more flexible and intelligent.

In some areas we need less freedom. There should be less freedom to pollute the environment. For example, to drive dirty and noisy vehicles in urban areas. There should be less freedom to hide your identity, both online and on-the-street. Issues of national and personal security need to be balanced against individual freedoms. There should be less freedom to make other people's lives a misery. We need better tools and sanctions to deal with anti-social behaviour. In this context the right to strike needs a wider debate. Where there is a monopoly provider of essential public services such as health, transport or utilities, then is the negative impact on others too great to allow a personal withdrawal of labour? And finally, we should focus on the rights of children. For example, the right to safety, care, education and healthy nutrition. As noted by David Goodhart: "Seldom are the needs of babies and children heard in the policy argument.".

Political parties will have different views on where the balance lies between freedom and control in each of these areas. They must let us know what these are. These views will then come with distinct policy choices that can be voted upon at elections. That will give a mandate for important policies which will not always be universally popular.

Contribution

Nothing feels better than helping people. Helping people to fulfil their potential. Helping people when they are down. Helping people to feel safe and valued. We want that for our society. Although we can be critical of them, this is what has brought most of our MPs into politics. We need to encourage and enable people so that they can contribute to society. We need to recognise and reward those that do. But at the same time, we need to work to break down the "entitlement" culture. A culture where people feel entitled, no matter that they have not contributed. A culture where people focus on their own rights, while ignoring or infringing the rights of others. The entitlement culture exists in all parts of our society. Those that are privileged are the most entitled of all. Just as we need to work to break down the mechanisms that embed poverty and a lack of opportunity, we need to work to break down the mechanisms that embed privilege. An effective tax system will be part of that. We expect the wealthy to give back as well as to receive.

A greater emphasis on citizenship, starting in schools, will help embed these values. Aristotle noted that the greatest means for ensuring stability of constitutions is the education of citizens in the spirit of their constitution. An education in citizenship will teach people what John Kennedy meant when he invoked his fellow Americans to "ask not what your country can do for you—ask what you can do for your country".

Education should be supported by the encouragement of community service for younger people and for older people. Companies and government can be leaned upon to create these roles. There are many useful jobs that need to be done. We can encourage this by developing attractive part time employment contracts for this type of work, and by recording and recognising the community, voluntary and caring work that people do.

Wellbeing

Our personal wellbeing, our happiness and contentment with life, is the most important thing that government can help deliver. The environment in which we live, our upbringing, our education, our friends, will have a big impact on the opportunities we have and the choices we make. These things will influence how content we become.

Our political parties have different views as to what is most important to national wellbeing. Labour stress the importance of equality, of sharing resources fairly, and the desire to help others. The Conservatives major on rewards from enterprise and the ability for personal improvement. Both have accepted the importance of free enterprise as a mechanism of generating national wealth to allow redistribution to take place. But there is more to wellbeing than these things.

Maslow's Hierarchy of Needs is a way to help understand the elements that go towards personal wellbeing. The "needs" are most often shown in a triangle. At the base of the triangle are physical needs such as food, water, warmth and rest. Then comes the need to feel safe and secure. At the top of the triangle are the more esoteric areas of belongingness, love, esteem, and finally, something called "self-actualisation". This is the ability to achieve your full potential. Political parties have tended to focus on the bottom of the triangle. In a developed economy we should treat a focus on these first two tiers as a given. They are what business call "hygiene factors". The basic service or product must work. Customers assume this to be the case. They choose on how they "feel" about the product or supplier, in particular, whether they trust it.

We should understand a politician's vision for our happiness when choosing them. Unfortunately, the "vision thing" has gone out of fashion in British politics. It has been a long time since Britain had visionary politicians. We must demand this of them. If we don't, there is a danger that politicians do have a vision, but they don't tell us what it is because they know we won't like it.

We hear much about changes in exchange rates and rates of economic growth, but the most important measure is national wellbeing. Various international bodies already measure this, but we need to agree on our own national measure. A measure to show how our people feel about their lives. In business, we had an annual staff engagement survey where we asked the same set of questions every year. These measured how happy and engaged people were in their work. We took this very seriously. The results allowed us to benchmark between years, and between departments and locations. We could identify hotspots for action. We published the results with an action plan. Woe betide a bullying manager, or the head of an under-resourced department!

A national exercise like this needs to be independently managed. It would be too important to put in the hands of government. This is a job for our head of state. A job for our new king. There is a national parallel. In 1972 the King of Bhutan introduced the concept of Gross National Happiness (GNH) for his country. This was later developed into an index. A "*King's Survey*" in the UK would measure the wellbeing of our people. The King would chair a committee of the K12 (composed of the heads of each of the UK's 12 devolved Kingdoms) where findings were presented and discussed. Representations would be made to the governments of the devolved regions, and to the controlling national parliament of the day.

Efficiency

In Britain, muddling through is a prized national asset and skillset. It is not something we should be proud about. We have so many MPs that they can't all fit into the debating chamber. Our second chamber is unelected, populated by the aristocracy and has-been politicians from a different age. Our head of state, God bless her, is over 90 years old. We have road networks that are clearly unfinished. Bottlenecks are everywhere. Traffic lights stay red while pedestrians that aren't there cross the road. We decide to build a third international runway at one of the most congested and polluted places on the planet. We invest billions to shave a few minutes off a train journey that most people can't afford to make. We have 46 independent police forces. Our taxation system is bloated and over-complicated, ripe for simplification and review. We are building on our green belt, but everywhere we look in our towns and cities we see empty or under-utilised buildings and space. Places where new buildings would improve the urban environment, rather than blight the rural environment. We build huge windmills in some of our most beautiful rural areas, but seldom in the industrial areas that use the power. Houses are disfigured by solar panels, while acre after acre of flat roofed warehousing, shops and offices are solar-free, but could be generating energy for their own use. BBC digital viewers sit through 10 minutes of wallpaper when the local news is on – inviting us to turn over, when that space could be used for advertising. In London, we see the army in fancy-dress for the tourists, while the police are guarding most of our public buildings, tooled up like ninjas. Can't the army do this instead? These things bother me.

There are hundreds of examples like this. If you have an appetite for them, you can read a 496-page book called The Blunders of our Governments, written by Anthony King and Ivor Crewe. Businesspeople look at these things and sigh. Our politicians don't seem to have the competence, the leadership ability, or the appetite, to get to grips with them. As Michael Bloomberg notes "Running government is an executive job… Unfortunately, no matter how smart you are, it shows if you don't have management experience."

It is ironic that politicians complain that business is too short term in its outlook, focused only on next year's profits and share price. In reality, those with the shortest time horizon are often politicians, worried about the next ministerial reshuffle or the electoral consequences of taking the tough decisions needed for the long-term health of the country. A democratic and reformed House of Lords will help. It will have a mandate to ensure efficient use of resources and efficient execution of policy. An important part of their role must be to better scrutinise both ministers and senior civil servants and to demonstrably promote better accountability.

6

PLANNING

There are two things in which well-being always and everywhere consists. The first is to determine aright the aim and end of your actions. The second is to find out the actions which will best conduce to that end.

Aristotle, Politics

National planning has fallen out of favour as a tool of government. Politicians and civil servants have lost this skillset and this way of thinking. John Bew notes that "Brexit has revealed that we have lost the habit of thinking strategically about our place in the world, of combining all our attributes together in pursuit of a coherent goal." Bew gives the example of Britain's considerable development budget – one of the biggest in the world – which remains detached from the broader goals of its foreign policy.

Planning promotes good government. It also promotes healthy democratic processes. It forces politicians to be explicit about what they want to do, and how they plan to do it. In recent years we have seen a breed of politicians that want to gain power, but then when they get it, they don't know what to do with it.

Planning is also important because there are some initiatives that only government can champion and make happen. We don't want a return to detailed state planning, nationalisation, or huge curbs on free enterprise. But UK government has relied too heavily on markets. It is too susceptible to lobbying and special interests. They have not set out adequate leadership, frameworks and national goals to help businesses and people to plan their own futures.

Brexit, wherever you stand on this issue, has shown the importance of planning. It has shown the importance of thinking through the implications of policy choices. It has shown the importance of getting your team behind a plan before you start to implement it.

Good government starts with a plan

This book proposes a legal framework, and a timetable, to make political parties produce coherent and comparable plans before a general election. This will allow voters to make informed choices. They will know for what they are voting. This discipline will also force parties to shape their policy ideas properly. Once a government is formed, everyone will know what is going to happen.

This process will allow us to see the different visions and plans from each of our political parties. Each party's candidates and members will have seen these, debated them, and signed up to them. This first stage of sense-checking and political buy-in is essential. Margaret Thatcher's laws brought discipline to the Unions. We need something similar for our political parties.

Democracy will then decide the path we take. With a more representative voting system, we will have a larger choice of political parties. Coalition governments will become more common. This can be a good thing. In coalitions, parties need to merge their plans, picking the most attractive and sensible policies from each. Bruce Mathers, in the Economist letters page, notes, "The dreary sort of continuity which can be produced by coalition governments would have served both Britain and America well over the last two years. Here in Switzerland, we have a permanent coalition, the dreariest continuity imaginable, and it is a big factor in our stability, resulting in long-term business confidence. Long live dreariness in politics!"

Forming a strategic plan

In business, a strategic plan will usually be developed through a series of "away days" where the management team go off-site to isolate themselves from the normal distractions of their jobs. This is a useful process to weld teams together and to form a common sense of purpose. The next sections walk through that process, as if we were producing a strategic plan for the UK. In an ideal world, each political party will go through a planning exercise like this - before they take power. The summary output will be put to the country as the essence of each party's manifesto.

Consideration of future trends

The planning process will start with some stargazing, contemplating the trends which will impact the future environment in which we will be operating. Policies and plans can then be formulated with an understanding of how things could change. Some of these trends and possibilities are outlined here.

Ageing populations in developed nations will present a challenge to public finances. But older people will be fitter, better educated, and more energetic than any of the older generations that have gone before them. Enlightened societies will help people to play a more active part in their communities as they get older, and to carry on working and contributing to society. Most people will move in and out of jobs, with their peak earnings being in their 40s or 50s. People will require retraining at different periods of their lives. Expert systems and voice recognition will revolutionise health care and education, as well as bringing challenges to professions such as law and financial services. Robot devices will challenge traditional manual jobs. But new consumer needs, new requirements and new ways of living, will replace these jobs with new ones.

Many consumer devices will become as good as they can be. Frequent up-grades will not be required. The return to vinyl is an example. High-end 1970s hi-fi sound as good, or better, than anything we have today. Manufacturing efficiencies and advances in robotics will continue to bring down the cost of physical goods and improve their availability. People will increasingly value experiences, personal well-being and development, over consumerism. The edges between work and leisure will continue to blur.

Modern communications already make it possible to work effectively from different locations. This trend will accelerate. The internet allows people to have the comforts of home wherever they are. People will be able to live anywhere, but still wake up and read a downloaded version of their preferred UK newspaper, watch the Premier League or the BBC, and have increasingly life-like internet enabled face-to-face conversations with their family and friends.

The global mobility of the rich and the highly skilled will need policy responses. The difference between the rich and other people is that they, and often their jobs, are mobile in an increasingly mobile world. They and their money will always be welcome in other countries. Governments will have to take care that they do not make these highly mobile lifestyle choices fashionable, or morally supportable, by crossing the fair and reasonable tax barrier.

State support will be tailored and targeted toward individual need. This will come at the expense of privacy as data from many sources allows extremely accurate personal profiles to be developed. There will be a reaction to this through the development of alternative lifestyles, and a yearning for a simpler non-digital world. With more information sharing and better understanding of the human genome we can expect further advances in disease control. But there will be uneven access to these medical advances.

Our environment and climate will be impacted by the vast increase in human population, economic activity, and accumulated pollution. Technology will help us to adapt but we will need to deal with the consequences of our past actions and to promote cleaner industries and energy. Air quality, climate change, biodiversity, and the management of freshwater provision will become pressing political issues. The world will continue to experience inequalities, conflicts, and famines which will put pressure on borders. Wide-scale access to internet information will fuel dissatisfaction with local life opportunities in disadvantaged or oppressed parts of the world. Migration, both legal and illegal, will increase.

Asia will continue its rapid economic development with China becoming increasingly confident, influential and assertive. India will leap forward. Africa will see rapid population growth accompanied by food and water shortages. This will create conflict and inequality and migration pressure which will be a challenge for Europe. But this huge market will also create large commercial opportunities. Many other parts of the world will see population growth stabilise, and then go into reverse.

Better battery technology and cheaper solar and wind generators will allow more energy self-sufficiency for communities and individuals. Sharing platforms will allow capital goods, such as cars, to be hired or shared rather than purchased. Vehicles will change to be non-polluting and increasingly automated. This will dramatically improve the quality of life in urban areas.

Expert systems will become more human-like with their own personalities. Superman's father came to life long after his death through a hologram programmed to talk, act and think like him. Systems like these will be with us sooner than we expect. Gaming technology and 3D goggles will allow experiences to be interactive. These devices will also enhance reality, in that people can look out at a vista and see how it was in times gone by, or how it will be once building development has taken place.

Digital assistance will be available immediately, always and everywhere. Complex processes like surgery will be performed remotely. Robot devices will be connected to skilled surgeons, who can reside anywhere in the world. Screen technology will become even more life-like and larger. Whole walls will be covered in screens. This will allow smaller spaces to appear larger, and for people to have immersive experiences.

Forming a vision

The planning process will then move on to discussions about vision. What sort of country do we want to be? That might then be encapsulated into a vision statement. These are a bit 1990s, but they can still be effective if you can come up with a concise vision that everyone can get behind. Something that can win hearts and minds. A vison statement for the UK could look something like this.

"The United Kingdom is a proud and independent nation with a culture and history of fairness, democracy, and doing the right thing. We strive to make a positive impact on the world through our creativity and freedom of thought, while valuing and enhancing our beautiful islands, and protecting and nurturing every citizen that lives here."

Deciding on objectives

The next stage of planning is to determine the objectives that will help to achieve our vision. Political parties will put different weighting on these. Socialists will put a high weighting on equality, social justice and community. Libertarians will put a high weighting on personal freedom. Ecologists will value sustainability and environmental protection. Capitalists will champion monetary wealth, free markets, and policies that encourage growth. We need all of these things, but at times we get out of balance. Too much growth can threaten stability, too much equality threatens entrepreneurialism, too much stability leads to corruption and a lack of dynamism. Occasionally, we need "creative destruction" to allow change to occur. That is why democracy is such a powerful force. The people decide when change is required.

National pride is also important. Our comparative performance against other nations determines how we feel about ourselves as a nation. History shows that we are a competitive country. That is a strength. When the game was empire building, we were very good at it. When the game was manufacturing, for a long time we were excellent at that. Global banking and services, we rocked. As the new games of the 21st century emerge, if we remain adaptable, we will be able to play them very well. Walter Bagehot knew this back in 1867. "A dead, inactive, agricultural country may be governed by an unalterable bureau for years and years, and no harm come of it. But if the country be a progressive, eager, changing one, soon the bureau will either cramp improvement, or be destroyed by it."

The methods by which we achieve our objectives will be determined alongside our values. For example, we can see that China has achieved huge economic development, but at the cost of democratic freedom and environmental degradation. We don't want to do that.

Assessment

An assessment process will objectively benchmark ourselves against other countries on a whole selection of financial and non-financial criteria. Are we a happier place, a healthier place? Are we sustaining our environment? How good are we at nurturing our people? Are our universities, businesses and creative industries world class? Are we winning at sport and competitive events? The planning process will include input from experts on competitor nations. We must look closely at other countries' strengths and weaknesses and at their business models as we plan our own future. Our foreign embassies will be an important source of insight.

There are lots of different management tools for helping an assessment process. The best known, and probably the best, is the SWOT analysis. SWOT stands for strengths, weaknesses, opportunities, and threats. A SWOT analysis for the UK is included as an appendix.

Action

Once an assessment and objective setting process is complete, then an action plan can start to be produced. Actions will focus upon exploiting strengths and opportunities and considering what can be done to fix weaknesses. The action plan will address perceived threats. Agreed actions from the plan will filter down into the objectives for each responsible executive. Executives will be appraised and rewarded on their achievement of these. This creates a "performance culture". This also ensures that everyone is pulling in the same direction.

An effective executive

A performance culture requires mentoring and regular one-to-one meetings for appraisal and feedback. The management effort that this requires means that it can only work when there are a manageable number of reporting lines. Theresa May had 21 direct reports. That is not conducive to good management, for team building, or for creating a performance culture. In business, the CEO is very unlikely to have more than ten people reporting to them. Five is a typical number for a high performing team. A reporting structure with just five reporting lines to our Prime Minister is possible. This would group government departments along the functional lines familiar in business; Finance, Operations, Marketing, Legal, and HR.

An allocation of our current Government Ministries and Government responsibilities along business lines would look like this. **Finance** will include Business, Industry, Science, Taxation, Standards, Pensions, together with statistics, purchasing, financial regulation, planning and reporting. **Operations** will include Defence, Energy, Transport, Digital, Food, Tourism, Border Control, The Fire Service and Housing, together with resource planning, standards, complaints management and IT. **Marketing** will include, Trade, Overseas Development, The Foreign Office, Immigration Policy, together with communications PR, benchmarking, insight, national branding, and the BBC. **Human Resources** will include Health, Education, Culture, Communities, Sport, Equality, The Arts, The Environment, Training, and Social Services. **Legal** will include Justice, Police, Prisons, Civil Liberties,

Control of the Civil Service, Security, Audit, Risk Management, Laws, and Brexit.

A reporting structure like this need not interfere with the workings of Cabinet Government. Big decisions can still be made with the benefit of full consultation. But in terms of the implementation of those decisions, and the important business of running the country, smaller executive teams will be more effective. In particular, every cabinet minister should have one to one supervision, support, and mentoring. That cannot occur in a structure which involves too many direct reports.

Cultural change

The concepts of a focused executive and of performance management will seem foreign to our politicians. But why can't Government be more business-like? Is it because we have too many egotistical politicians that are unable to work in teams or take direction? People like those described by Aristotle. "People who enjoy too many advantages – strength, wealth, friends – who are both unwilling to obey - and ignorant of how to obey any sort of authority - and only know how to rule as if they were masters of slaves." Or is it because, as the Economist suggests, "Tribunes of the people have been replaced by professionals who make their livelihood out of politics. The trouble is, it turns out that politics is not a very attractive profession and therefore not attracting enough good people."

The Blunders of Our Governments outlined, in grim detail, the hugely expensive consequences of the endemic bad management in our Governments. In their concluding chapter the authors, Anthony King and Ivor Crew, conclude that "if the incidence of blunders is to be reduced, it is the British governing system and the ways in which people function within that system, that needs to change." King and Crew's impressively detailed study of blunders made both of them far more sympathetic towards radical change than they were before they started out. Unfortunately, because that hasn't happened, they will have plenty more to write about in the next edition of their book.

Conclusions

Much good will come from the stability and certainty of a balanced budget, the beauty of a protected environment, the comfort of a caring community, and the confidence of a long-term strategic plan. In a rapidly evolving world - with powerful competitors - our gift for muddling through is not a good substitute for competent leadership and planning. Good planning will promote confidence and better government.

The UK has some strong comparative advantages. Our relatively small surface area and our high density of population means that we get a great return from infrastructure spending. Our single language, respect for national institutions, lack of corruption, and strong national identity mean that we should be able to move quickly when we need to. Our national ability to change, and to give our government a democratic mandate to do so, will be key to shaping ourselves to succeed in the future. Government has a responsibility to organise and plan - and to engage our best minds in this debate and in this task. A well thought out strategic plan will be an essential tool to help us position ourselves to cope with the fundamental changes in demographics, climate, technology, power structures and personal aspirations that the UK and the rest of the world will experience in the years ahead.

7

POLICIES

Imagination is more important than knowledge. For knowledge is limited to all we know and understand, while imagination embraces the entire world, and all there ever will be to know and understand.

Albert Einstein

This part of the book focuses on policy ideas, grouped under nine headings: community, finance & taxation, transport, overseas development, education, health, defence, business, and national projects. There are some new ideas, some old ideas reformulated for a modern world, and some borrowed ideas. Some ideas will appear strange. Some will not stand up to scrutiny. Others will seem like the most sensible thing to do. The strangest way of doing things is often the way we do things now. Who would ever think to invent The House of Lords, a constitutional Monarch, hereditary peerages? Who would design a United Kingdom where Scotland, Wales and Northern Ireland have devolved decision making powers, but England does not?

In the world of modern political unions and e-democracy envisaged earlier, each policy idea will need to fight for credibility on a policy formation website. Each policy idea will have to find backers and supporters. The bad ones will be thrown away, the good ones will be refined and marketed. We will have a free market for new ideas. Many of our Government policy blunders could have been avoided if policies first had to prove themselves in this way. Policies would not be adopted or implemented until they had first been fully worked up and tested by experts, and by the people that work in the areas they affect.

Existing political parties, or new ones, are welcome to cherry pick from these ideas. Beatrice and Sidney Webb, two early Fabians, believed that the best way to change our country for the better is to permeate all of its parties, left, right, and centre, with new ideas.

Community

We were proud at how we managed the Olympics. It was as though we had regained our wartime spirit. The country united and celebrated. It was uplifting. The physical infrastructure of our participating cities was tidied up: they looked modern and bright. Britain showed itself off to the world. The volunteer Games-Makers were a revelation, showing diverse and friendly faces. We got to see our armed forces providing security in a most efficient and friendly way. This was "Community Britain" at its best.

We do community well in this country. It is one of the reasons we love living here. Whether our sense of community is based on our neighbourhood, family, school, choir, place of worship, football team, work, pub, or our clubs and societies, we do it well. Our open-heartedness and our sense of a common bond binds us together. Our communities give us friendship, a place in the world, and a sense of worth and security. They are our rock in times of adversity.

We also do integration well. For ten years I worked in Croydon. At the beginning, as I drove to work, I noticed that children were walking to school in their ethnic groups. Now I see a complete mixing. Croydon must be one of the most ethnically diverse places in the world. People get on fine with each other. My own children don't register someone's ethnicity.

Politicians sound awkward and bogus when they talk about community. Most of them have a narrow or limited experience of living in the places where these things really matter. Successful and busy people tend to live in "bubbles" with other successful and busy people. But communities are important. Politicians should ensure that their policies support them, or at least do no damage. The policy recommendations here focus on engendering a sense of community, generating civic pride, recognising and rewarding those that do community work, and encouraging and helping people to be more engaged in their communities. The emphasis is on the state as facilitator rather than provider.

A sense of community

The foundations for our sense of community are developed in school. Children need to be taught British history and values and the concept of citizenship. This can be done using common video and internet modules, and with the help of external speakers. Shopping far and wide for school places is time consuming and stressful. It cannot be good for so many of our children to have to travel so far to school. We want children from the same communities learning and growing up together, forming local friendship groups that will last a lifetime.

Vibrant and up-to-date town internet sites are a good place to discuss local issues and to make available those people who are responsible for local services. They can also advertise local events and clubs and societies. Because these sites are so important, central government should set minimum standards for them. They should audit these sites to ensure local governments are meeting them.

Pubs and markets need to be encouraged and protected with favourable tax treatment. Pubs lie at the heart of British culture. Many are struggling and typically pay 40% of their overall takings in tax. Gyms and similar organisations that provide group classes and are open and inclusive also need support.

Playing for or supporting local sports teams gives people a feeling of belonging. A visit to Newcastle on match day demonstrates the importance of the local football team to the community. Local representative sports are an important part of building and strengthening community bonds. Competitions between local communities are a good way of bringing communities together. Be it sport, music, or art – representing your community engenders a sense of pride. Splitting England into "kingdoms" will facilitate more local competition to take place. Government should work with each of the national sporting bodies to ensure that local leagues and competitions are in place and are coherent in respect of community structures. There should be a target to arrest the decline in sports participation in Britain. Particular attention needs to be paid to the fall in sports participation amongst the poor.

Festivals and carnivals are another great way to bring people together. Local government should help to make these things happen. Regional government should make sure that they do, registering and advertising all such events. Community celebrations and events are important; they get us to meet each other, they make us happy, and they make us feel that we belong. Events such as half marathons, cycle rides, and arts and music festivals help build community. Local themed events such as Hastings Pirates Day and the Petts Woodstock music festival are fun, distinctive and inclusive.

Civic pride

Some British towns and cities have "let themselves go". They do not demonstrate civic pride. We know the symptoms. Ugly and brutal architecture, poor quality public spaces, and housing in poor repair. High streets that are depressing, with a preponderance of betting, pound and charity shops. This is not Britain as it should be. These communities need help to improve themselves. The section on constitutional reform gives some suggestions as to how this might occur. The King's Survey will identify hot spots of unhappiness. Action plans will be developed, and central capital expenditure and assistance provided. Today we spend £14bn every year on overseas development, with no noticeable return for UK citizens. We need a fund like this to develop the infrastructure and facilities of our own down-at-heel towns and cities. Investment from which we will see the benefit year after year.

There is a huge imbalance in public amenities between communities. For example, public park land and playing fields, swimming pools, golf courses and libraries. Government should set standards for the minimum provision of community facilities. It can measure and compare these. We should have standards for important things, like public toilets, public seating, waste bins. The average distance from a local school. The amount of allotment space per person.

Community branding is important. Attractive and well cared for town signage, uniformed service personnel, clear maps for visitors, clean parking facilities and train stations. These things reflect well on a town. Hotels know the importance of impressive "on-boarding" process. The importance of making those first good impressions. Towns need to show their best side to visitors, engendering pride from their inhabitants. My hometown, Hastings, is a great place to visit, but soon after passing the "Welcome to Hastings" sign, which is currently dirty and overgrown, you encounter a traffic jam. There is a terrible right-turn junction which blocks the road. Not really a good welcome at all.

Some towns need to identify and to promote their unique selling points. Every town has something to be proud about. Not all of them tell you what that might be. Some areas may not be lucky enough to have good public buildings or go-to landmarks or attractions. National institutions such as the lottery fund should help with funding or support to build some. The Eden Project in Cornwall shows that, with help, regions can develop new and interesting places to go.

Ugly buildings, badly maintained buildings, and empty buildings will blight towns. Towns and citizens need to have stronger powers to put these things right. Many of the ugliest buildings belong to the local council. Citizens must be able to petition Regional Government for buildings that blight their environment to be demolished. Rectification will be enabled by a National Blight and Rebuilding Fund. Rectification Notices will be issued where buildings have been left to deteriorate. These will give owners time to put the situation right. If this does not happen, then redecoration teams will be employed by the community to do the work. An interest-bearing charge for the cost of the work will be put against the property. This will be redeemed in priority to other charges when an eventual sale takes place.

Recognising community service

Records are kept of the bad things that people have done, e.g. driving convictions, credit defaults, drug offences etc. We should also record the good things that people do. We should have a system of Community Credit. Volunteer and service organisations will register with their local authorities. They will apply to have roles accredited for community points. An annual return will list the people that have filled these roles. Service will generate points. These points will be called Community Credit. The caring professions and frontline services will also generate community credit. Teachers, social workers, ambulance drivers, nurses, soldiers etc. will earn community credit in addition to salaries. We will also recognise non-paid carers: those looking after children or loved ones that need help.

A community card will store these points. These will be similar to credit cards. There will be different levels of these. For example, a person who had been a lolly-pop lady for many years might end up with a gold card. These cards will allow preferred access and discounts to events and services. These are the people that will get up-graded on air-flights. These people will have high social status. This might be rewarded and reflected in public service provision (e.g. access to the best council housing) and in mitigation when someone gets into trouble (e.g. more lenient sentencing). There is also the potential to issue negative points for anti-social behaviour.

Community credit will trigger awards and recognition. Community medals, county medals, and kingdom medals. A lifetime of outstanding service will be recognised by a national honour, awarded by the king. But most importantly, community credit will also generate a tax-free community dividend. This will be paid to those with active and historical community credit points – with higher levels paid for current points. These dividends will be partially funded by fines. For example, parking fines, speeding fines, pollution fines, criminal fines and regulatory fines. These amounts could be significant, for example, the £34 million fine recently paid by Goldman Sachs and the £183 million fine levied on BA for a data breach. This system will make the bad people pay the good people. What better way to inject money directly into our communities?

People will also be encouraged to make bequests, knowing that their money will go directly to the people at the sharp end, those that are helping to make our communities better places to live. And at times of recession, governments may also use this network to make special dividends to help stimulate the economy. Economists term this type of policy "helicopter money", but this helicopter will only drop money to those people in our society that are doing their best to improve it for everyone.

Mobilising our senior citizens

There are many jobs which need to be done. Yet we have an army of capable people that we are paying to do nothing. This is our older population. We won't be able to continue this indefinitely. We have a demographic time-bomb. We have large unfunded public pensions' entitlements. The age when pensions are payable is already being pushed backwards. That is likely to continue. One thinktank suggested that 80 should be the age for the public pension to start. What are people supposed to do for income between the ages of 60 and 80? What will they do with their time if they have no disposable income? We need to create more opportunity for older people to work in their communities, and to continue to earn. This will help keep them active, fit, and visible. Work will also give them important social interaction. Everywhere I look I see useful work that needs to be done. There is a staffing crisis in all parts of our caring services. And yet we have this army of often bored and forgotten people. Many of these people are currently being paid – through pensions or welfare – for doing nothing. That is not good for them, and it is not good for us. As a society, we would get more back than we paid in if we mobilised our older people. How would we do it? One part of this will be the establishment of the limited hours "grey contracts". This initiative is outlined in the Business part of this chapter. Another enabler will be the establishment of Community Support Groups for our older people.

Community Support Groups

At the age of 60, and then again at the ages of 65, 70, and 75, people will get a letter from their council asking whether they want to enrol in a Community Support Group. A positive response will trigger a visit from a Community Service Partner (CSP). This person will collect information about life experience, skills, health, and ethnic and religious background. They will generate a personality profile using psychometric testing. Using this information, the CSP will form balanced local community support groups. Each group will contain 12 people. The parallel is anti-natal support groups. These groups work superbly well to help form networking and self-help groups amongst people who are at the same life-stage. My wife still meets with her anti-natal group some 29 years after it was set up. They are a firm group of local and supportive friends. Our old people should have this type of support as they face the challenges of aging.

Once the group has been determined, the CSP will own it. They will return to brief the group about the paid part-time community service roles that they will be able to do. A list of potential jobs will be provided and allocated according to skills, experience and health. Each person in the group will be given a tablet device connected to the internet. This device will connect to a hub, giving useful training and support. The device will also connect the group to each other, by a type of Facebook, or by Facebook itself. Next will come a facilitated meeting of the support group. This will happen at a local premise designated for this purpose. This could be a community hall, a church, or maybe local pubs or restaurants. Members of the group will be designated specific roles within it. For example.

1. *IT* - help with tablets, PCs, mobiles, internet, and social media
2. *Financial* - help with finding the best local deals, internet shopping e.g. insurance, electricity, telephones, credit
3. *Health* - liaise with and understand local NHS services, access expert health systems
4. *Exercise* – advice and organisation
5. *Nutrition* – advice on diet and vitamins, group buying of local produce
6. *Education* - organise lecturers and book clubs, liaise with local colleges and schools
7. *DIY and security* - help to fix things
8. *Transport* - help to organise journeys
9. *Catering* - run cooking classes, prepare meals for people temporarily incapacitated
10. *Social* - organise day trips, social events, advise on holidays etc.
11. *Mental health* – helping to fight depression, pet sharing
12. *Gardening* – help and information in respect of gardens and local fauna and wild-life

Those with similar roles in other groups will be put in touch with each other to form functional networking groups. They can share ideas and best practice. Meanwhile, each community support group will continue to be facilitated and evaluated by the CSP until each group has bonded and is functional. If people do not like their groups, or if someone is not fitting in, then some counselling or shuffling between groups will be facilitated by the CSP.

Finance and taxation

We all want good public services. With this desire must be a recognition that we will need to pay for these services though taxation. In recent years we have not been raising enough in taxation to do this. We have been paying for many of these services through debt. It has been said that Britain has an addiction to debt funded public services. This way of living makes me feel very uncomfortable. As Bill Bonner observes, "we have moved our debt to future generations. This worked when each successive generation was reliably richer than the one before it. But this generation has made no financial progress compared with the previous one. However, we have lumbered them with substantially more government debt."

We need to have an honest debate about the level of public services that we want - and can afford. This will be difficult if those that demand more spending are not prepared to be honest about the taxes that will need to be raised to pay for them. We cannot continually get by on the never-never. Governments that try to do this risk losing the trust of the markets, and the voters. An important prerequisite for an economy to prosper is trust and confidence. If we have trusted politicians with a credible and attractive plan for our future, with fair taxes and well-targeted public expenditure, that will give us all confidence to keep investing, the confidence to keep spending. A credible plan, and confident politicians promoting it, will stop people from worrying.

Our country is not going to be isolated and poor. It is going to be sustainable, diverse, vibrant, and wealthy — wealthy in the things that make life worth living. As you age, you are not going to be a burden on the community, miserable and poor. There will be fulfilling jobs for you to do, vibrant communities to live in, neighbours to help. There will be people to care for you when you need it most. If you are young, you can look forward to several different careers. Your life will be full of opportunities.

But for us to look forward to this future, we cannot remain addicted to debt, and addicted to growth. The two things go together. We can only keep borrowing if we assume that we will have more income in the future to pay it back. That drives all sorts of strange policies, for example, the UK's rapid population growth through immigration. Before the Brexit vote there was a school of thought that we should invite in lots of extra people to pay extra taxes to pay for our debt. And, yes, in the short term that did work. With a larger population our national income increased. But as individuals, our growth in income was a lot less impressive. And those extra people need housing, and eventually they need to be looked after themselves, adding to our debt rather than reducing it. That then requires even more growth. Cramming more and more people onto our already crowded islands is not what we want. What we want are policies that achieve sustainability, equity, and quality of life.

National accounting

We want to devolve power to 12 British regions. We must have a uniform method of seeing how they are doing. We can do that by agreeing a standard form of annual reporting. The parallel is a business's annual report. In America these are called Form 10-K. An example of what a form-10 might look like for a nation has been produced for America by Microsoft's ex CEO Steve Ballmer. This can be seen on the website USAfacts.org. These reports will identify cash inflows and outflows for a region. They will record each region's strategy and objectives. The reports will make explicit subsidies between regions, and average spending per person on local services. Central Government will report on the activities for which they are responsible, for example defence, planning, taxation, standard setting and overseas relations.

Tax allowances

The emphasis of recent governments has been to stop people from paying income tax by increasing the tax-free personal allowance. This insulates many people from government tax decisions. The policy is also inefficient. This allowance is not targeted at the poor. It is income related, not wealth related. The spouses of high earners get the full benefit of this relief, as do asset-wealthy older people. It is commonly used by the non-working spouses of high earners to shelter investment income. A better approach is to scrap the tax-free personal allowance. Replace it with a lower rate of starting tax - and allowances targeted at specific groups of people. The first allowance will be a Citizen's Allowance for British nationals. This will recognise the benefits of income being reinvested back into our communities. Where we need to employ foreign nationals in vital caring industries, such as nursing, then we will have a Key Industry Allowance. Similarly, a Seasonal Allowance, for people we need from abroad to help us to harvest our crops. If we are short of physics teachers and needed to attract them from overseas, we can attract them in this way. But we should not be subsidising temporary migrants who come to make our sandwiches or our coffees. These jobs should be done by our own people, or not done at all because of automation. Higher skilled roles will be higher paid, and if the employer really needs them, then they can pay the higher wages to make up for a higher tax take.

National insurance

National Insurance (NI) is an antiquated tax. It was supposed to build up a fund to pay your pension, but the government spends it like any other tax. There are two types of National Insurance. Employee NI (EENI) is paid by employees. Employers' NI (ERNI) is paid by employers. The amount that employers pay is based on the number of people they employ, and how much they pay them. Every employer, small, large, worthy or unworthy, pays ERNI on the wages they pay their staff. This is called a pay-roll tax.

Governments see NI as an "invisible tax". If they scrap it, they will need to increase other, more visible, tax rates. That is a poor reason to keep it. Organisations that give people work are vital to the economy, to communities, and to the individuals they employ. We should not tax this activity. We should scrap both EENI and ERNI and collect the lost revenue through the income tax system. This will be a large change to our system. It will require some transition rules. Employers will be required to rebate their ERNI savings to their staff as a one-off salary rise. The thresholds between tax rates will need to be adjusted to recoup what is lost through removing NI for higher earners. This can be sweetened by allowing deductions for "averaging" from the top rate. Earned income at the highest rate can be averaged over the last 3 years to mitigate high rates of tax on "lumpy" earnings streams.

Tax relief

The removal of NI will mean that more income is collected through the income tax system. That will make it important that we review all available tax allowances. As Phillip Inman in The Observer notes, HMRC offers some 1,140 tax-relief schemes. These schemes cost £100 billion a year. Their complexity means that they favour companies and individuals with the greatest wealth. Not many businesses could survive by allowing their customers to choose how big a discount they were going to make from their bills. But that is how our income tax system works. People can reduce the income tax they pay - to nil if they want, by using tax allowances. If you are wealthy and donate all of your income to the donkey sanctuary, then that is a good thing to do, but should the Government then refund the tax you have paid on that income? Surely it will be better for them to give it to the teachers and the nurses.

Pension saving costs the exchequer over £30 billion a year. A higher rate taxpayer gets a larger pension subsidy from the government than a basic rate taxpayer. The same principle applies to charity donations. A higher-rate taxpayer will get a greater subsidy than a basic rate taxpayer. A standard allowance rate, at the basic rate, will be more equitable. We also have expensive personal tax allowances for certain types of personal investment (EIS and SEIS). We would be better off by scrapping these, and using the money saved to support business in other ways.

Finally, all tax allowances should be accounted for as government expenditure. We should know how our money has been used. For example, where we give tax relief on donations to overseas aid, we should include this as part of our Overseas Development Expenditure.

Inheritance tax

Young people should not be expected to pay back the huge government debt built up by their parents. They won't be able to, they shouldn't have to, and they won't want to. Their parents will need to pay it back themselves. That will be through inheritance tax, and through taxes on the sale of their houses. Nobody wants to pay inheritance tax. The thing that makes this bearable, is that we won't be around to see it happen. There is only so far that we should go in allowing wealth to cascade down generations. But these capital taxes must not be used to fund current expenditure. There is a case for hypothecation.

Taxes on spending

Large internet retailers damage our high-streets and encourage imports. Some of them have corporate structures that shelter them from tax. An internet sales tax will balance things in favour of local retailers. Shops contribute to communities in many ways, including through employment and by paying property rates. Other countries do this, for example, India has a 6% internet shopping tax.

Insurance Premium Tax (IPT) is now at 12%. This tax has become a soft target for Government, raising close to £5 billion. For businesses, IPT is a dead cost since unlike VAT there is no offset against sales taxes. Insuring your home or business are a responsible choice to protect against catastrophic loss. They should have a lower rate of IPT than vehicle insurance.

Environmental taxes

There should be more tax on activities that damage the environment. These would include taxes on activities that damage the beauty of our countryside. An example would be a tax on electricity pylons located in areas of natural beauty.

National Payment Agency

A large amount of casual, cash-based, work goes unrecorded and untaxed. One tenth of Britain's economy is thought to be informal. We need this informal economy. It helps to get jobs done that need doing. Much of the work is supportive and caring. We don't want to make it harder for this work to be done. But we can set up a supportive system to record and regularise it. We can do this through a National Payment Agency (NPA). Every citizen will have the right to hire out their labour on their own terms. But payments for their work must not be made directly to them. They must be made to a government agency that will collect the money on their behalf. Appropriate tax will be deducted before payment is made to the worker. This will simplify and regularise the process of hiring out your labour. This will also help small "one-man band" type businesses. These businesses often do not fulfil their potential because they are reluctant to take on paid help. There is much effort required in setting up a payroll, and additional responsibilities from hiring staff. Small and early-stage businesses will be able to use NPA accounts to pay staff. This valuable dispensation will need controls in place to ensure that exploitation does not take place. At some stage staff will need to become formally employed, and to obtain employment rights.

The NPA system will use national identity cards. This will make it more difficult for illegal immigrants to join the informal jobs market. The UK will become a less attractive destination for illegal immigration.

National Pension Scheme

We will replace National Insurance with an optional money purchase pension scheme. This National Pension Scheme (NPS) will work alongside the state pension. It will work in the same way as privately-run defined contribution schemes. In these schemes you get tax relief on contributions and the money is invested to create a fund for you to use in your retirement. Private schemes will always have their place, but alongside them we will have a government run scheme. The money in this scheme will have limited invested options: Infrastructure Bonds, Property Bonds, UK Champions, and a UK stock market tracker. Administration will be outsourced to existing private pension providers.

Infrastructure Bonds will be guaranteed by the government. They will pay an indexed-linked real return – say inflation plus 1%. The money will be invested in ring-fenced national infrastructure projects that create an income stream. For example, funding a nuclear power station, a tidal energy scheme, or a new airport. This funding will be "off balance sheet" as far as the Government is concerned. It will not add to our national debt. We will avoid the embarrassment of having to ask the Chinese to fund our infrastructure. Property Bonds will use incoming funds to purchase Government owned and occupied buildings. The Government will pay a commercial rent. National UK Champions will invest in iconic and important UK companies. Businesses that we want to keep out of the hands of foreign investors. Companies like Rolls Royce, BP, and of course Cadbury, had this not already been sold to the Americans.

Any UK based organisation, company or individual could choose to use this system. It will do away with the burdensome concept of "work-place pensions". It will also generate large amounts of money for investment in UK infrastructure spending – investment in UK Plc that will help us generate more income in years to come.

Public sector pensions

Civil servants value their final salary pensions. But their cost is very large and conveniently opaque. We need to tackle the problem. To remove the benefit from existing workers and retirees would be wrong. This was part of the terms on which they accepted the role. Instead, we need to bring in change gradually starting with new joiners. We also need to cap the benefit to high earners. The current final salary scheme must remain in place for new "front-line" roles, e.g. in the NHS, the Forces, teachers and social workers. And yes, for constituency MPs. But we must cap the salary to which it can be applied, say, to £40,000. For salaries beyond that cash contributions will be made to the NPS. Those in non-customer facing roles will not automatically join the final salary scheme. These staff will initially join the NPS, outlined above. This will put these staff on a par with people doing similar roles in the private sector.

Transport

Back in the day, society tolerated smoking in public places. A whole series of industries relied upon it. Today the thought of smoking in a busy restaurant or on the train seems incredible. Surely, in the future, we will look back at the way we have tolerated the unrestrained use of motor vehicles in the same way as we now look back at smoking. Cars, vans and lorries are choking the life out of our cities. Parking is using up huge amounts of land. A significant proportion of our national and personal income is used to buy vehicles that stand idle for 90% of the time. These are usually hugely over-specified for the task.

Noise pollution is an important issue in densely populated areas. Some of the noisiest vehicles are high powered motorbikes. Urban living would be hugely enhanced without air and noise pollution from vehicles. The benefits to the quality of life in urban areas of quiet electric vehicles cannot be overstated. These will allow a higher density of housing and allow residential accommodation in places that would be intolerable to live in before. If we lead the way in the UK, we will benefit from better and healthier cities. We can also benefit our balance of payments if we can establish UK manufacturing of clean vehicles to replace these dirty, noisy, old war horses.

Investing in roads

These new types of vehicles will still use wheels. They will need to use a road network which is eccentric, inefficient and incomplete. We need to complete the job. Too many dual carriageways peter out into archaic single-track carriageways. Too many scenic towns and villages are blighted by traffic. Too many disadvantaged towns suffer from the lack of decent roads to them. Bottlenecks are everywhere.

Investing in roads, bridges and tunnels creates jobs and promotes development. Any driver in France cannot help but be impressed by the quality of the physical infrastructure, including so many wonderful bridges and tunnels. It is to our shame that we put up with such shambles on our small island. We need traffic engineers to examine where jams occur and to recommend how to alleviate them. The widespread use of satellite photography and digital maps has revolutionised transport planning and control. We can see where traffic jams occur every day. This can help transport planners to determine where resources are best used to make design changes to help improve the flow of traffic.

Technology

Speed limiting technology has been around for a long time. Mopeds have devices inside them that cap their speed. Soon every new vehicle will be fitted with a device like this. This change will gradually alter the nature of our car fleet, reducing the excess capacity of engines, making them more efficient. It will also make the average cost of new vehicles cheaper. But the change should be accompanied by a long over-due increase in the speed limit on motorways.

The ability of a limitation device to know where it is opens the potential for it to vary its speed cap according to time and location. For example, during school hours we could limit the top speed of cars around schools to 20 MPH. Cars will become connected to the internet and become part of "the internet of things". This will allow speed limits to be reduced when the weather is poor, and increased if there is little traffic, particularly at night. This technology could also be used for road pricing. The safety and cost benefits are compelling. We can do away with speed cameras and road traffic police and save lives. Driving will become less stressful as the car controls its own speed.

Driverless vehicles will struggle to navigate British roundabouts and country lanes. But stretches of motorway should have dedicated driverless lanes. Car satnavs will give the option of going into driverless mode on these motorways. They will join a convoy of vehicles going at the same speed. This will allow relaxation or work while in the convoy.

Standards

Hydrogen fuelled vehicles offer a non-polluting alternative to petrol or diesel vehicles. Government can help this form of fuel to gain acceptance by insisting on hydrogen refuelling points at supermarket and motorway service stations. Electric vehicles need a standard size for slot-in rechargeable batteries. These will work alongside a vehicle's base unit battery. Owners will lease removable "get you home" batteries. They can drive into a petrol station and swap the discharged battery for one that is already charged – so no delay. And these batteries will be recharged off-peak. Electrically assisted bicycles have huge potential. These vehicles allow longer commutes. Once rain protection is provided, electric assisted bicycles could become the default choice for many journeys. Government can help by producing standards for battery sizes so that these can be mass produced. They can also ensure that office buildings, shops, and restaurants provide adequate bicycle parking facilities. They can choose a British made machine to equip the police.

We also need standards for the frequency of places to stop and take a break on dual carriageways and motorways. We need inspection and standards for service stations. Some of these reflect very badly on our country.

Vehicle sharing

Once the take-up of ride hailing apps like Uber becomes ubiquitous, the need for your own vehicle will reduce substantially. A vehicle to hire will always be a few minutes away. But it will be important to make sure that this type of service is available to everyone, including the old, the sick, the poor, and the technologically illiterate. Access to a fleet of shared vehicles will be valuable for the NHS and other government bodies. As the biggest employer of them all, government can lead the way.

Junction review

Many of our junctions are badly designed. It seems that motorists must be punished for their use of polluting vehicles in urban spaces by making them stop and start all of the time. Bottlenecks are accepted as an inescapable fact of life. Urban planners think of road building in urban areas as like dredging a furrow in a sodden field. Each new road is immediately filled to overflowing. New roads promote new journeys, and therefore their impact on congestion is limited. But this type of thinking does not recognise that in future the vehicles travelling on these roads will be quieter, safer, more intelligent, and non-polluting. We should make our urban roads work better for them.

Every local authority should have a periodic traffic review by independent traffic-flow experts. This will cut through local politics and inertia. A report will be produced for the next level of government and for local consultation. This will highlight improvements that can be made. Some of these will involve the compulsory purchase of land and the rephasing of traffic lights. Most improvements will be simple stuff. Where a vehicle on a busy road makes a right turn into another road, the road should always be made wide enough for vehicles to pass on the left. Bus stops should always allow room for traffic to pass on the right. In some cases, new bridges and tunnels might be recommended, or a significant redesign.

Better junction design in urban areas could also save many deaths and injuries. At busy T junctions the vehicle about to join the traffic could sit in a car sized "box". Cyclists and pedestrians would cross behind the vehicle in a lane delineated by a "speed table" at the same height as the curbs. These "bicycle bridges" will slow cars before they enter the box. Cars will be required to slow down and look for cyclists and pedestrians before crossing the bridge and entering the box.

Lights, cameras and humps

We should not stop cars on red lights at deserted junctions in the middle of the night. We should not use average speed cameras to enforce 50mph speed limits on roadworks when the people working on them are safely tucked up in bed at night. Traffic lights and speed enforcement devices must become intelligent, calibrated to have different settings depending on the amount of traffic and the time of the day. This will speed journeys at off peak times and reduce energy use and frustration from unnecessary stopping and starting. Speed limits should increase to 85 on motorways outside peak hours. This will regularise the faster cruising speed seen on the outside lane of motorways.

Speed cameras should always show the speed limit they are enforcing. Many average speed cameras do not do this. This is a particular feature of Scottish speed cameras. There are miles and miles of them on A roads and dual carriageways. Is the speed limit on these roads, 50, 60 or 70? They assume you know. Visitors crawl along slower than they need to, stressed that they might be breaking a speed limit they don't know.

Speed bumps cause pollution, noise, and vehicle wear. They encourage the purchase of large SUVs that can roll over them largely unimpeded. They cannot turn themselves off at night. They cannot turn themselves off for police cars or ambulances. They can damage peoples' backs. They will still have their uses, but smarter cars should be accompanied by smarter ways to calm traffic.

Road charging

The number-plate recognition and charging system that operates at the Dartford Crossing can be expanded to different stretches of road. The greatest users of the roads should be the biggest funders of them. Road use charging can generate the fund for road and junction improvements. It can also be accompanied by liberalisation of speed limits outside of peak hours. Foreign heavy goods vehicles must pay an appropriate fee for wearing out our roads, and for the pollution they cause. We can agree subsidies and rebates for people, where justified e.g. for disabled drivers, carers, and for those working in our essential services.

Serious road accidents

There are two sets of victims of motoring accidents: those that have suffered damage and injury, and those caught in the resulting congestion. Most of us have experienced severe delay in traffic jams caused by motorway accidents. We should strive to do better. The cost of these delays is enormous. Serious accidents on motorways should be declared "national incidents" and dealt with by a specialist fast response team. This team will be part of our armed forces. It will be a specialist elite force trained for all road accident eventualities. It will deploy military hardware, planning, communications and resources. In particular, heavy lift helicopters and battlefield medical care and extraction.

Cycling

Provision for cyclists in the UK is poor. If children want to cycle to school, they must use roads. They will share these with lorries, vans, busses and motorbikes. Cycle lanes might give the impression of safety, but they often do not provide it. To achieve safety cyclists must be physically separated from traffic. If there are no safe cycle lanes, then cyclists should share pavements rather than roads. This should be the default position. Where there is not room for this to happen, the path can be delineated for walking only. This proposal will be controversial. There is a dangerous speed culture in UK cycling. The key to the safe mixed-use of footpaths will be the control of cycling speed. Also, the teaching of protocols for the safe passing of pedestrians. Compulsory cycle training at school will include a code of practice for safe and polite cycling in areas shared with pedestrians.

Cycle speed limits on paths need to be represented as a multiple of walking speed. Cyclists and children will find this concept easier to understand than miles per hour. So 1x would indicate walking pace, 2x would indicate twice walking pace. Some pavements could operate like bus lanes, with rules to allow certain types of cyclists, at certain times of the day. Speed limits will apply and be enforced. There might be places where cyclists are required to slow to walking speed. Some pavements might be "one way" at certain times. During the school day - say from 10 until 3 – pavements could return to pedestrian only use. This will allow an ample window for elderly people to have sole use of the pavement.

High speed commuters will use the roads as before, with the requirement to wear helmets and to pay a cycling road tax. This will be at a lower rate if they also pay road tax on a car. They will be required to display detachable registration numbers. These will include an electronic identity fob which will be automatically scanned at intelligent junctions, and by the police when necessary. Normal traffic fines and points will apply.

Cyclists should benefit from some traffic rule exemptions. Making cyclists sit on red lights sucking up car fumes when the road ahead is clear is not sensible. At pedestrian request-stop lights cyclists must always slow down to 1x walking pace. They must always give way to pedestrians. But they can time their approach to pass behind a pedestrian while they are on the crossing. At some junctions they should also be able to turn left on a red light. This rule applies for cars in much of the USA, except that it is turning right on red in their case.

Air travel

The UK's international air transport hub is London. Each of its airports acts in isolation. It will be a more effective hub if we invest to make better connections between its airports. London will be the type of hub where you stay over. You can see the sights, do some business or shopping, then continue the journey, maybe from a different airport. When travellers fly into any of these airports, we must make it cheap and easy to stay over. A seamless transfer of luggage will allow travel between airports with just hand baggage. The receiving airport will store these bags. Over-night stays of these kinds will be VAT free. For business meetings, rather than force visitors to leave the secure area, we should allow local businesspeople to go through security to come and meet them within it. The more facilities we can provide within an airports' secure area the better. Not just first-class retail, but also over-night accommodation, gyms, cinemas, theatres, museums, nightclubs, and business meeting areas. London will become the business meeting capital of the world. It will take advantage of its favourable geographic position. Americans can meet here with Chinese. Africans can meet here with Russians. Then all parties can visit the theatre or a football match. A new airport to the East of London will complete this city-wide transport hub to all parts of the world. A new Eastern Airport will be focused on flights to the economically growing Far East market. Heathrow will be focused on flights to The Americas. Gatwick on flights to Southern Europe and Africa. Stanstead to Eastern Europe and Russia. West goes west, south goes south, and east goes east. This will minimise the number of flights over urban areas.

Having regular direct flights to economically important areas will give us a huge business benefit. It will make us easy to do business with. We will be a good place to locate a head office or a research centre. This development will also be good for tourism. These airports and routes will help people to come here, and it will also help us to get to other places. Individual airlines and airports cannot make this sort of vision happen. Governments can. That's what ours should be doing.

Rail travel

Train ticketing is complicated and unfair. If you pay for your ticket in advance and miss the exact train you have booked, you lose all your money. You can't be late, but the trains often are. Making train journeys comfortable, productive, affordable and reliable should be a greater priority than making journeys on them faster. The money for the HS2 initiative would have been better spent on enhancing local networks into and between city centres. It would have been better spent on buying some carriages with double decker seating. This would increase capacity and allow lower seat prices. The French know how to do this.

Overseas development

In 2015 UK Parliament passed the International Development Act. This commits us to spend 0.7% of our national income on overseas aid every year. In 2018 that mounted to £14 billion pounds. In 2015 Britain was the second largest donor in the World, behind the USA which gave 0.17% of its national income in this way. Proportionately, we spent over 4 times more than the Americans. We are a global leader in giving money away. We have seen the international influence and goodwill this has earned us during the Brexit negotiations. None. Zilch. We would have been in a stronger position, and more respected, if we'd invested the money into our armed forces. Not that I am suggesting that.

There are many things wrong with this policy. The absolute amount given away is huge. This spending leaves less money for the destitute, ill and uncared for people in the UK. Our taxes should be spent on things that help our people. There are arguments for why overseas aid can do this, but they should not be mixed up with charity. Politicians should not use law to commit subsequent governments to their preferred course of action. At elections parties should put forward proposals in this area to be voted upon. That will allow voters to decide which policy they favour. Governments can then decide how much is affordable each year given the domestic situation at the time.

Our Government spends more than it earns every year. For us to apply this policy we need to borrow the money to then give it away. This is the most expensive form of virtue signalling ever invented. It's as though every year we take out a loan and use it to impress our friends by making extravagant bids at charity auctions. Eventually we won't be giving aid, we will need to receive it. Many of us remember the humiliation of the IMF bailing us out in the 1970's. If state and public-sector pension commitments are included in our national debt, it comes to £4.8 trillion. That is a debt of £78,000 for every person in the UK. That doesn't feel like a wealthy nation to me.

Targeting expenditure rather than outcomes is a guarantee of inefficiency and bureaucracy, maybe even corruption. Much of our money is passed to third party agencies. If we must spend this money, we should spend it ourselves, rather than giving it to other organisations to spend on our behalf.

The multiplier-effect

If government spends money in a community, because that money is then spent on economic activity within that community, the impact is multiplied. For example, if you give £10 to a homeless person, she might use it to buy food from a grocer, who would then use this money to pay staff, who might then use it to visit the theatre. The theatre might then use this money to employ actors, who would spend the money on rent etc. etc. Money goes round-and-round in a community, multiplying its impact. So, when we give money outside our community, or in the case of Foreign Aid, outside our country, we lose this potential domestic multiplier benefit. The same thing happens when migrant workers remit money to their home country. The money remitted, estimated at £8 billion, leaves our communities and can no longer work its multiplier magic within them.

Reallocation of the foreign aid budget

Proposals to reduce the foreign aid budget will only gain support if they are accompanied by commitments to use the money saved for good purposes. For example, to help solve domestic poverty, which is a pressing need. Professor Philip Alston of the United Nations reported in November 2018 that 14 million people, a fifth of the UK population, live in poverty. He will no doubt be very supportive of plans to help solve that problem in this sensible way. The policy proposal in this area is to revoke the International Development Bill and commit to spending half of its £14 billion annual budget to eliminate homelessness and rough sleeping in the UK. That will still leave £7 billion annually to be spent on international development. That is seven thousand million pounds – every year. This remaining budget will be spent in more focused and effective ways.

World class disaster response

The best type of overseas spending is when we help another country that has encountered a disaster. We give lifesaving help that really does make us walk taller in the world. Let's make sure we are as good at this as we can be. We should also make this expertise available internally. Our reaction to the Grenfell Tower disaster was a national humiliation. A branch of the military should provide this capability. The ability to put boots on the ground and to organise a swift coordinated response resides here. We get there quickly; we get there first. We get there with food, helicopters, hovercraft, earth moving equipment, engineers, generators, search and rescue teams, reconnaissance drones, communications, and medical teams. These are the sort of invasions we must plan for. In the case of very large disasters, that is a good use for our new aircraft carriers. This work will keep our military on their toes, leverage their fixed assets (e.g. helicopters) and build capability that will also be helpful in war situations.

Overseas development areas

Hong Kong was the first of the Asian Tiger economies. A small region was made semi-autonomous with free port status and British standards of law, education and policing. Its 427 square miles became a huge growth node for the region. The area was eventually returned to the Chinese. Disney purchased a great deal of land in a most unpromising swamp-like area of Florida. They then built Disneyworld, bringing infrastructure, jobs and tourists to the area. The development helped Disney, but it also helped Florida. These approaches are worthy of study. Let's not spread our money around with only vague expectations of a return. Let's focus. Go for a win-win result for Britain and the host country.

Pakistan gets the most British Aid, some £351 million. Could we not use that money to lease or buy an area that can be developed through trade and inward investment on a win-win basis? Pakistan has 307,374 square miles of land. A region the size of Hong Kong would represent 0.14% of the country. The same approach could be adopted in Ethiopia (£334m), Nigeria (£253m) and Sierra Leone (£214m). That will be four counties to focus upon, nicely distributed across developing regions. If we add another African country, further south, that will give us five Overseas Development Areas.

We will bring our ways of doing things to these territories. Our income tax and VAT systems, our currency, our policing, our corporate structures, English corporate law. A lease would specify the right to have a free press and non-discrimination of religions or gender. These are the things we are good at, not building runways. Tax revenues will be remitted back to the host country.

Our universities and schools will set up both English speaking and local language off-shoots, with the same educational courses and qualifications as in England. The same with our museums, art galleries, and theatres but with local content and performers. We will set up some modern teaching hospitals.

There will be security issues, but these will need to be confronted. We will work with the local people and institutions to overcome these. It will be the local people that will be working in these growth nodes and institutions. We are not looking to set up gated English communities, just to provide opportunities and structure. These centres will help the host country by providing educational training and qualifications. There will be investment in infrastructure and a stable and safe environment for business development and for tourism. Tax revenue will be generated for the host country.

One important win for us would be an agreement that we could use these hubs to house people that have claimed asylum in the UK. Currently these people reside in Britain while their case is being examined; many go missing. We can also outsource some of our public service work. On-line health consultations and diagnosis can be performed from Pakistan. We can set up specialist centres for hip operations, allowing people to choose to fly out for this option to skip the queues. Rather than bring overseas doctors to the patient, we can bring the patient to the overseas doctors. Countries with warm winter climates, once safe and healthy, will make attractive retirement, convalescence and tourist centres.

Some people will see this as colonial and arrogant. But it doesn't need to be. The key is to work up our plan with the country concerned, and to have a long-term contractual relationship. We are not forcing our money on any country. This time we want to put in, rather than take out. And let's face it, can we really point to a return on the many billions of pounds that we have been spending every year in traditional ways?

Education

My parents were teachers in state schools. I know what a taxing job it is. My father taught maths in a secondary modern school. He described it as standing on stage for 6 hours a day in front of a hostile audience. But it can be tremendously rewarding. Good teachers can massively influence people's lives for the better. Teachers need our support and respect, and to be listened to. Government has meddled too much over the years. Yet our educational system and institutions, our teachers, remain a huge national asset. Many of our educational establishments are world class, particularly our universities.

Support

One of the themes of this book is that people's working patterns will change. Many will have more than one career. Support will be needed to retrain for different roles. Most people will be refreshed and energised as a result. Reduced hours roles, particularly to suit older works, can help the teaching profession. Experienced teachers, as they age, will be encouraged to move to "later life contracts" with reduced hours, and no loss of pension benefit. This will keep their skills in the profession and avoid early burn out. These people will be supported by "later lifers" moving from other jobs and retraining to become teachers. Potentially a new teacher at 60 on a reduced hours later life contract could teach for 10 years or so. We will bolster these additional teachers with an influx of trained coaches and mentors for our children. These people might also be later lifers with all the maturity and life experience they have to offer. We will then begin to match the best pastoral care that our fee-paying schools can offer. Every child will have a school granddad or grandma, their own personal coach. These people will be trained and paid and will also be recognised with Community Credit. They will work alongside our teachers.

Internet teaching

Facilities like YouTube allow the best and most engaging teachers in the world to come into our classrooms. Teachers must be helped by structured access to a national library of such material and to interactive on-line learning modules. This is the way that Citizenship courses will be taught, to make sure that everyone in the UK receives the same knowledge and teaching about the important things about our country, and their responsibilities and rights as a citizen.

Learning records

Each UK citizen will be provided with a Learning and Development Record. These will be Facebook type internet records owned by the individual, but with secured access to the institutions that are providing learning. Learning records will be secured by blockchain. Public examination results will be recorded here and accessed by third parties confidentially and securely. Schools and nurseries will automatically set up these records for each pupil. Individuals will decide to what extent these records will be made public to potential employers, to parents, and to mentoring organisations. The site will produce standardised CVs to a high standard for potential employers and universities. This will level the playing field so disadvantaged children will have CVs as polished as middle-class children. These accounts will also incentivise children and later life learners to accumulate marketable qualifications and experience.

Expert careers advice

Learning records will interact with an expert system developed to provide careers advice. Job descriptions and requirements, for every job in our economy, will be known by the expert system, alongside the training, aptitude and qualifications required to do the job. Videos will be recorded of people that do each of these jobs. They will explain what the job involves and the satisfaction they gain from doing it. Through a series of questions, using the benefit of artificial intelligence and machine learning, the expert system will be able to match people to potential careers. It will provide advice on the type of training and development required to do them.

Military Training Certificate

Twenty-three thousand children leave school every year without a single qualification or GCSE pass. Some children rebel against an "academic" environment. In doing so they hamper those that are more inclined to learn. They take up a disproportionate amount of teacher time in discipline issues. We should try a different approach. My father-in-law talked fondly of his two years of national service. He spent most of his time in Egypt, where alongside being shot at, he played a great deal of sport and learned discipline and respect. He also learned how to read. We should look again at this concept, distil what was good, cleanse what was bad, and see whether we can re-invent it for today's world.

National service experiences are the sort of things that middleclass kids now seek through gap years and organisations like World Challenge. We know that fee paying schools distil discipline and respect. There is a thriving market for "military fitness". Why should we deny these types of things to poorer children? Rather than make military service a compulsory duty, we should make it into a valued experience resulting in a qualification. For some children a normal school-based environment is not working. Let's try something different.

One of the most important things with national service is that participants are taken away from their home environment. That will be challenging for a modern 14-year-old. There will need to be a great deal of support. But we can do this. Upper-class children have been leaving their families for boarding schools at younger ages than this for many years. Many will come from troubled families and neighbourhoods. A controlled, disciplined environment will help their education and personal development. Army sergeants already note the remarkable change in the disposition and ability to learn of young people bought about by regular healthy meals together with exercise. That's what these guys will get.

There will need to be plenty of pastoral care available on site, with each child allocated a trained adult mentor. There will need to be controls and inspections in place to guard against physical, mental or sexual abuse. These should not get in the way of tough and fair military discipline when it is required.

The first year would focus on fitness, discipline and practical education in a military environment. Citizenship, diet, health - including sexual health, respect, and basic life skills will be taught. And they will go to bed at regular times. They will want to, because they will be tired out, and because they will need to get up early in the morning for their run. Early morning runs are what many successful chief executives do, why not our children too? The second year will move to vocational training. There will be work-streams teaching practical skills. Things like bricklaying, plumbing, farming, car maintenance, plastering, childcare, care for the elderly and nursing. Skills for which there is a ready market, but which our current educational infrastructure is not well set up to provide.

Once the MTC course is completed there will be a passing out ceremony. Some participants will move into full time forces roles. For those that don't, there will need to be continued support and mentoring in the community.

Britain already has a good reputation for education overseas, so once these structures and qualifications had been set up then they could be "exported". A British Military Training Certificate could become a valued and recognised qualification worldwide. Britain does not have a monopoly on directionless kids.

Working in the community

An important part of a school's role is to prepare children for work. Work experience is already part of a school's curriculum, but finding these roles is very hap-hazard and entrenches class divides. What chance does a child have of getting work experience in a solicitor's practice, if one of their parents doesn't already work in one?

Businesses must make these places available by law, and schools should determine the most appropriate candidates to take them up. In agricultural communities', work experience should include farm work. School term times can be planned to allow pupils to help get in the harvest. We are not suggesting Mao's Cultural Revolution, but it should be a fun and educational part of a child's school life to learn from where our food comes. To know what it feels like to have a hard day's work in the fields. In times past, city workers used to have their holidays picking hops in the Kent fields.

Universities

Our universities are a huge national asset, spearheading research, and training our best minds. But do they provide value for money to their students? Are they providing a supportive environment? Universities must publish service standards for their students. All students must get regular seminar "group discussion" meetings once a week. They must get a one-to-one meeting with their tutor every week. A written progress report, to a national standard, must be posted on their on-line learning and development record at the end of every term. Students must complete feedback forms on the quality of their lecturers and tutors. There must be a clear referral processes for when things go wrong.

Students and employers' value one-year qualifications. There should be more of these. Most degrees could be completed in two years. One-year and six-months courses, particularly in IT, languages, and technical subjects, must be available. These are attractive to older people and to overseas students looking for a useful gap year experience. We should offer guaranteed state funding of the first year of a university course for those with at least 5 years at a state school that have achieved the minimum qualification requirements. Funding will not be available for those from fee paying schools.

The business of education

This is a rapidly growing global market. Foreign students need to be welcomed and cherished. They bring with them money and skills. Once qualified, their knowledge and hopefully their affinity and fondness for Britain will bring all sorts of lasting benefit. We have a comparative advantage in this field. We are the home of the English language. Where better to learn it, or to perfect it. We have some of the world's most prestigious educational institutions whose qualifications are valued worldwide. We are a welcoming and open multi-cultural country with resident communities from around the world. We are an interesting place for young people to visit, with a cultural vibrancy and rich historical legacy.

Health

The NHS is faced with many challenges, not least from the ageing of our population. As people get older, they need more health care. Change is difficult due to the scale of the organisation, the number of interest groups, and the politicised nature of the debate. Businesses faced with these types of problems might decide to bring in strategy consultants. These people look at problems from afresh. They talk to people from all sides and produce non-political and factual reports. These reports include recommendations for change and improvement.

A Royal Commission

An exercise like this could be set up under a Royal Commission. These have gone out of fashion in the UK in recent years, although they are still used in Australia. The last Royal Commission into the NHS was commenced in 1975 and reported in 1979. Before commencing a new Royal Commission, we should review previous Royal Commissions in the UK, and look at how these exercises are conducted overseas. A Royal Commission on Royal Commissions if you like. A world connected by the internet allows for better processes than have been used before.

Public consultation

The British public feel strong ownership of the NHS, so must be involved in the consultation exercise. Staff, unions and local authorities must also be consulted. All interest groups will be asked to contribute to a consultative website. This will be a public "data room" where facts and submissions are stored. Nothing about the exercise must be secret. The data room will map out the structures of the NHS, its costs, and its processes. It will look at all aspect of service provision, mapping out processes for someone with a heavy cold, to someone diagnosed with a terminal illness. It will ask for submissions from those that use the service. It will review bureaucracy, recruitment, purchasing, buildings, and the use of technology. It will benchmark all aspects of the NHS against other countries' health models.

The initial process must be rigorously time boxed. We will then have a period of introspection and debate while the data is reviewed. Three different consultancies will be asked to work independently to produce recommendations for change. Interested parties will record their views, ideas and experiences against these recommendations on the website. These reports will then be submitted to a cross party committee for review. These sessions will take place behind closed doors to avoid political grandstanding. The committee will decide on which recommendations they agree upon, and areas where there is political disagreement. The Government will take forward agreed measures. Areas of contention will form differential political or regional offerings put forward at elections.

Regional diversity

The consultancies will be asked to outline the aspects of our health model that should to be common – e.g. purchasing, IT and HR - and those aspects of our health service where different regional models are possible. Health provision is an area where the kingdoms will be able to take different approaches, while not losing the benefits of national economies of scale and specialism.

To facilitate different regional delivery models there will need to be a central funding formula. This will be based on the size of the population, adjusted by age and local wage and property costs. Some regions might then choose to boost services through higher local taxes. Some might choose to improve delivery through an element of pay by use. This will give more diversity, and a more politically accountable and flexible local service.

ID systems

Identity cards and systems must be the passport for the receipt of public services, particularly health services. Technological advances allow us to identify individuals accurately from their biometric data. This might include the facial recognition systems at airports, fingerprints, iris recognition, dental records and DNA. We need to start collecting this information from birth. In 2009 India set up a cloud-based ID system that holds the details of over one billion Indians. The system is called Aadhaar and records fingerprints, iris scans, name, birth date, address and gender. It logs this against a twelve-digit number. Simple fingerprint recognition systems now unlock many public services. The government believes that it has already saved $5bn.

In the case of accident, people's medical records will be immediately available. These ID systems will also make the workplaces of NHS staff more secure. Only authorised people will be given access to hospitals. Those that have a history of violence or abuse will be quickly identified. This system will be controversial and will require controls. But the potential benefits are huge. It is reasonable to expect the customers of public services to identify themselves in this way. India has shown that it is technically feasible.

NHS Active

Regular exercise improves fitness and well-being and reduces the need for later life health interventions. Yet for many people taking exercise is not part of their life. Doctors and health professionals should be able to prescribe exercise. This will require an infrastructure of personal fitness advisors and NHS fitness centres. Ideally, these will be in town centres close to public transport. Doctors will then review the amount of exercise done before resorting to drugs, particularly anti depression drugs. Once a person has been kick started on the route to a healthier lifestyle, most will then want to build fitness into their lives.

NHS on the high-street

Patients want easy access to NHS services. Short lets on vacant high street premises will help, in a similar way to how charity shops operate. Non advised NHS services can be supplied from these premises e.g. kidney dilation, blood testing, skin cancer checks, blood pressure checks etc. We can also use vacant premises for NHS fitness centres.

NHS Overseas

Rather than importing care staff and doctors, for some simple types of operations where there are queues, e.g. hip operations, we may find it cheaper to export patients. People will be given the choice as to whether they want to skip the queue in this way. Production-line centres, focussed on certain types of medical intervention and care, would be developed in our Overseas Development Areas - supported by our overseas aid. These will be NHS standard hospitals, also available to local people, and staffed by well-trained local doctors and nurses. As part of their training, many of these local staff will be able to enhance their earnings and experience by working for periods of time on contract in the UK.

NHS on your PC and smartphone

The future of diagnosis is expert systems. Speech recognition and the use of speaking and thinking avatars online. These experts will use learning decision trees to identify the likely causes of illness. Patients will be able to consult these cheaply, with the benefit of blood, urine and blood pressure results obtained at high street health centres. Expert systems will have an option to break out to online consultations with real doctors when all symptoms and measurements have been collected and the system has identified a range of possible outcomes. These doctors can be based anywhere – for example, in South Africa. The NHS is uniquely positioned to produce an expert system like this. This can then be licenced around the world. The NHS brand can also be leveraged in many other areas, e.g. the development of vocational training qualifications and standards.

The right to die

I watched my mother fade away with Alzheimer's over a very long period, cared for by my father at home up until the end. The last few months were distressing. She would not have wanted this for herself. I don't want this for myself. There are well-reasoned and passionate viewpoints on both sides. But ultimately, this should be a personal decision. We should have the right to decide when and how we end our own lives. If we are to have human rights legislation, then this should be in it. We can frame safeguards to protect the young, the vulnerable and the depressed.

Eighty two percent of the public back assisted dying. Our MPs don't agree with us. In 2015 MPs voted on plans for a right to die in England and Wales. Seventy four percent of MPs voted against this bill. This was one of my motivations for commencing this project. When I cast my vote, I want to make sure that I am voting for a candidate that will back the right to die.

Drug use

The Royal Commission will consider our approach to drug use. Many countries treat addicts as patients rather than criminals. Should we allow controlled access to the least harmful and addictive types of recreational drugs? There may not yet be a national consensus. This could be an area where our kingdoms take divergent approaches.

Medical records

Patients must own their entire medical and biometric record, securely available on-line. A good model is Britain's online tax return system. A set of standards are published for data download and upload. Third-party system designers can then produce NHS approved "My Health" systems that people can chose to store their data in a user-friendly way. This will encourage us to take more personal responsibility for our health.

Defence

We have a fantastic military tradition, but we seldom seem ready for the new battles. We expect our foes to fight in the same way as they have before. Our arrogance is our weakness. Like support for our football team, we believe we are best, until we get into competition and find that we are not. Some of our defence decisions look as though we are repeating these mistakes. That we are investing to fight the last war rather than the next. For example, our huge expenditure on vulnerable assets like aircraft carriers, and on out of date delivery systems such as Trident. We need a clear view of what we are defending against. Where our threats will come from. Prestige hardware will not protect us from terrorism and cyber- attacks.

In a world where traditional jobs will become scarcer our forces will be an important source of recruitment and training. They should be more integrated with communities and society, and bolster and support the work done by other agencies. We should grow our force numbers and source equipment locally wherever possible.

Trident

Trident ticks all the wrong boxes.

- ✓ Fighting the last war
- ✓ Expensive, bespoke, and difficult to build
- ✓ Long timescales to deliver
- ✓ Foreign technology
- ✓ No export sales potential
- ✓ Vulnerable trophy asset
- ✓ Potential rapid obsolescence through new weapons technology
- ✓ Huge financial vested interests
- ✓ Political, not military decision

The debate around the renewal of Trident was narrow. If you were anti-Trident you were portrayed as anti-nuclear deterrent. That is wrong. In a world where your enemies have nuclear weapons, we need to have them too. But we do not need to spend so much money on a vulnerable, over-specified and out of date delivery system. Satellites, listening devices, and drones make it very hard to hide things anymore. Gone are the days when a battleship could hide in a Norwegian fjord. Large physical assets such as Trident submarines will be taken out quickly by adversaries with any degree of technical sophistication. And each one is enormously costly.

A sophisticated enemy is going to see missiles fired at it from a submarine. Anti-missile missiles will take our missiles down. We need sneaky and diverse ways to deliver these weapons for them to be a deterrent. In today's world of drones, miniaturisation and driverless vehicles, there are much cheaper and more effective ways to deliver a nuclear payload. The deterrent we need is the ability to deliver a small nuclear device exactly where we want it, in a way that our enemy cannot see coming. Britain does not require a doomsday capability like Trident. No country is going to threaten the UK in isolation with a nuclear strike. We are just not that important in the world anymore. The reason we have Trident is that we are paying tribute, not to the Vikings, but to the Americans. This is our contribution to the US nuclear shield. But the cost is now too high.

Aircraft carriers

In a fighting war against a technically advanced nation, these ships will be sunk. As Putin says, they represent a "convenient target". It will be impossible to defend them for long against drone, missile and torpedo attacks. The loss of life and the cost to our national morale of a sinking would be huge. It was a mistake to build such large and expensive ships. Smaller platforms are the future. But now that we have these carriers, we should be proud of them. They show that Britain has not lost its military mojo. They will be useful at projecting strength and power overseas, and as a substantial contribution to multinational forces. They can also promote Britain's soft power, helping with disaster relief.

Equipment sourcing

Many countries use their defence budget to help promote their home-grown defence industries. That's what we should do. We are currently a very open market to foreign suppliers. Both strategically and economically we must ensure that our British defence industry remains healthy. We must not lose the capability to build our own equipment. We should shape our defence effort around what we do well. So, if we can't build great tanks, we should focus on building and buying weapons that can disable them.

Equipment specification

In recent conflicts around the world the most popular type of military vehicle is a truck with a gun welded to the back of it. Most modern conflicts use cheap fast-moving vehicles. Many of these are converted from civilian sub-frames. We should build some of these. Inexpensive vehicles that can boss most 21st Century conflicts. We are fortunate to have one of the world's best manufacturers of construction vehicles on the planet in JCB. Let's give them a chance to make some military vehicles for us. We could get a lot of these type of vehicles for our money and there is potential export market. Some of these vehicles could be remote controlled or autonomous.

British invention

Q in James Bond, with his array of cunning devices, is an accurate caricature. Given a military problem, we are good at finding innovative solutions. We can harness this innovation. Disruption is occurring in methods of fighting and weapons systems. The Chinese approach to building a stealth ship - is to make it semi-submersible. It sinks like a submarine when it needs to hide from radar or missiles. Drone like hoverbikes get troops safely over minefields and difficult terrain. ISIS dropped hand-grenades into Humvees using commercially purchased drones.

The Swedish Goltland submarine costs $100m to build. That is the same as it costs to buy a single F-35 fighter jet. It is so stealthy that in 2016 war gaming tests it was able to "sink" the Ronald Reagan aircraft carrier time and again. Imagine the weapons our boffins could design if let off the leash. What is the modern equivalent of the midget submarines that sank a battleship in the Second World War? Let's be the innovator, rather than the expensive follower. Spending so much on foreign trophy assets starves British industry of research and development funds. Investment that could be helping to develop new, affordable and marketable defence assets.

Robots and drones

Intelligent robot control allows cheap consumer vehicles to be turned into effective weapons. Jet-skis can move at over 70mph, are highly manoeuvrable, and can be made into torpedoes. A driverless low-profile jet ski would be difficult to stop. Many of these could be programmed to work together in a swarm attack. To move in a way that makes them difficult to hit. Some might just be cheap decoy drones, weaving around aimlessly. But which ones? One hundred of these could be dropped over the side of some old tugboat. Expensive missiles can take some of them out, but how many of these expensive missiles will each ship have? If just one kamikaze robot wasp gets close enough to sting, it can disable a billion-dollar ship. Italian mini submarines sank two British battle ships in the Second World war. On land, a similar thing can be done with quad bikes. Drones are the threat now. The day that a swarm attack is demonstrated will be the day that 90% of existing "death star" type military equipment will be made redundant. If there is another war, this time let's make sure that we have the U-Boats and the blitzkrieg vehicles, not the dreadnoughts and the cavalry.

Forces in the community

It was a pleasure to meet our armed forces when they helped at the Olympics. It would be good to see more of them, working alongside our other services. For example, why do we have armed police in our airports and protecting our public buildings. Wouldn't it be better if the army did this? They can also perform other protection duties. This would free up the police to do the traditional police work that they are trained for. We should challenge the demarcation lines between forces. We can also leverage our military assets more. From using heavy lift helicopters to help with serious traffic accidents, to setting up fitness courses, to helping train our young people. The more active we can keep our forces, the more likely they are to be in a good working order when we need them.

Forces representative of the community

One of the themes of this book is that people should expect to have several different careers over a lifetime. This applies also to the armed forces. Career paths need to be built out of the armed forces, e.g. into the police, but also into them – for later-life recruits. Dad's Army has given people a bad impression of the potential of older people in military roles. Many older people are as fit as youngsters, often considerably fitter. And in modern warfare, machinery removes the premium on strength. Most front-line roles today require presence, wisdom and diplomacy. If we have to fight a shooting war, let's not put our youngsters in the way of that. Put the oldster battalions in the frontline. They have been tested by life. They know when to keep their heads down. They know how they will react when the chips are down. Some will welcome the opportunity to go out in glory. Rather than Dad's Army, the Grizzly Granddads and the Tough Mothers might be the scariest fighters around. The Kurds have shown what an effective fighting force an all-female brigade can be.

Recruitment

Outsourcing military recruitment to Capita was a mistake. They have a lengthy and bureaucratic process. No sensible people-based organisation would outsource recruitment. Your people are your biggest asset. You need to make sure that you get the best. Recruiting for attitude is vital for our armed forces, not a box-ticking skills assessment.

National Incident Force

We should deploy our military resources in real situations, rather than have them training on simulated incidents on some deserted heathland somewhere. Our response to the Grenfell Tower situation would have been better if the military had taken charge. For serious incidents we need a force which can bring authority, equipment, trauma care, and site recovery to bear. A force with fantastic communication equipment, trained and able to take command and control. A force that will do this quickly and professionally.

Business

There is a desire within the country for us to make more things, to grow more things, and to become more self-sufficient. That desire does not sit well with globalists, international bankers, and free market economists. But to those that value communities, self-sufficiency and harmony, it will sound pretty good. This section outlines the ingredients for a national plan for business that will raise standards and productivity and improve dialogue, particularly around regulation. This will include measures to help promote British businesses and to encourage domestic sourcing from them. Any national plan for business must address how we can get more balance in the balance of payments. Also, more regional balance. The plan needs to address skills, infrastructure, regulation, and strategically important sectors such as science, education and the media. Statistics on imports and exports, regional performance, and benchmarking of all types must be included.

Our trade deficit

British people love imports. We like to drink imported wine and beer, to drive foreign cars. There is no longer any stigma in buying foreign products in preference to our own. Government policy and example have encouraged this. If there is fair trade, and we buy more from them, and they buy more from us, everyone wins. But unfortunately, other countries are not buying as much from us as we buy from them. We make up the difference by selling assets to them, like London houses and British companies. That cannot go on forever. The right to buy imports should be earned through working. Through making and selling stuff ourselves. We must pay our way in the world. If we don't, there will be a reckoning. Maybe that reckoning will come when we have sold our last Mayfair property to the Russians, our last utility company to the French, our last chocolate manufacturer to the Americans, or our stock exchange to the Germans. It will be the young that inherit this situation; a country mortgaged up to the hilt for Prosecco. To avoid this situation, we need to attack our trade deficit. That deficit was close to £40bn in 2016. We need to export more - but that adjustment will take time. While this happens, we must find ways to import less. Ideally, by substituting home-made alternatives for imports.

Protecting the brand

The British Union Flag is one of the most recognised flags in the world. It gladdens and surprises me to see people from other countries wearing it. They wear it in France, they wear it in Italy, they wear it in America. The Union Flag is worn all over the World. It is pleasingly fashionable, but people also wear it because it means something, something beyond just our national symbol. Some of this meaning is associated with the Commonwealth, and those other nations that share the union flag with us. But the flag also represents brand values: democracy, diversity, creativity, and friendly relationships between sovereign nations that share these values. "British values," as represented by the Union Flag, are something which people from around the world are happy to buy into.

We are fortunate that our national flag is so recognisable and warmly regarded. It is a valuable and precious inheritance from those that have gone before. Every company and country would love to have a global brand like ours. That also means that we need to protect it. We need to ensure that goods and companies that use it, really do reflect our values. This starts with registering and certificating all "Made in Britain" goods and services. The not for profit organisation "Made in Britain" understands the importance of this. It has incorporated a modern Made in Britain trademark. Where companies use the word "British" in their title, for example British Airways, Government needs to take an active interest in their service standards and their values.

Tourism

The business that government does own, is tourism. We want people to come here. We need them to spend their money here. Production by robots will mean that most physical goods will get cheaper. People will value "experiences" over "things". Overseas travel will be a large part of this. British people know that, they are enthusiastic tourists to other countries. We can pay for this by welcoming foreign tourists to our own.

Britain as an attractive, welcoming, and interesting place to visit, is also an attractive place to work. A good place to site a business. Knowledge working is the future. Quality of life will be vital in deciding where knowledge workers choose to live. Britain is already good at tourism. There are many reasons people visit: history, culture, music, education, scenery, sport – we can tick pretty much every box, other than reliable sunshine. But we do have plenty of fresh sea air, a valued luxury if you are holidaying from the smog and heat of Beijing or Delhi.

We want tourists to go home with a wholly positive experience. We want them to roam throughout our beautiful islands, rather than just focusing on our already busy hotspots. That's where Government comes in. We need world class "on-boarding" at airports and ports. When people arrive, don't make them queue at under-staffed customs and passport control. Staff to get people through quickly. Make a name for ourselves as the best country in the world at which to arrive. This speed of entry cannot be at the expense of security. Technology can quickly collect iris patterns, facial records, and fingerprints of all arrivals. These can be matched with leavers. We'll know who is still here when they shouldn't be.

Focusing our hub airports on different regions can help shape what they look and feel like, and the services they offer. We can benefit from the people from these regions that have chosen to make the UK their home. They can be employed to welcome visitors in their own language.

A Welcome to Britain App will help visitors know what to expect and help them to plan to get the best out of their trip. On leaving, we can use it to collect information about the quality of their stay. Once completed, an emailed letter of thanks could be sent, signed by the King. This could include a picture of the visitor with the Royal family, created using the security picture of the visitor taken on arrival.

Promotion of British goods

We must give British and local companies a fair chance. There are good reasons, other than just our trade balance, to promote localism in buying. For ecological and community development reasons buying local is a popular trend. Preston's "buy local hire local" initiative shows what can be achieved. Government can help this trend by identifying where to buy British and locally produced goods. A Government sponsored internet site could work like Amazon, with advanced product search tools to connect local buyers with locally produced goods. If after a product search, no British produced product exists, then government can highlight this as a gap, and as an opportunity.

Regulation

Economists are concerned about our poor record of productivity improvement. One reason for this is our increased regulatory burden. We play by the rules, and these rules have become more extensive. Regulation, risk management, and HR processes get more attention on British boards than innovation, research and development and technical training. Meanwhile, unrestrained capitalism is working quite well in those ex-communist countries that don't care much for these things. A generation of our senior managers have built their careers on Power-Point presentations. The cost of the compliance industry that feeds these meetings is enormous. Government must engage with companies, regulators, and shareholding groups to reduce this overhead.

Protecting our iconic brands

We have many iconic brands. These are national assets that need protection. Any attempt at a foreign takeover of an iconic brand must be referred to a National Brand Committee. This could refuse a takeover or impose terms. This would protect national iconic brands such as Cadbury.

National projects

One of the themes of this book is devolution, for responsibility and power to be devolved to the lowest level. But there are some areas for which National Government must remain responsible. This section collects policy ideas for these areas, and for some important national issues that are not covered in other areas of the book. These are: jobs for older people, public service, housing, our environment, identity and personal data, infrastructure, technology, policing and the BBC.

Increasing job opportunities for older people

Longer lives will result in a greater number of older people, at the same time that lower birth rates are giving us proportionately fewer younger people. More jobs will need to be tailored to meet the needs of older people. These jobs will be attractive if they are part-time, allowing older people to remain in the jobs market, but also to have more leisure. The "grey jobs market" will be for people between the ages of 60 to 75. These people will already have had a working life to build up some security. Most of them will have got over their child supporting years. Their income needs should be reduced. But many will still want and need a job to fund the lifestyle they want and to keep themselves active.

Government can help this jobs market to develop by developing a special form of employment contract for older people. We'll call that a "grey contract" here. The working day for a grey worker will be one hour shorter than a regular worker. The working week will be 3 days. This will allow a job share. To make these contracts attractive to employers there will be two benefits. Firstly, the contracts will be for a fixed term – to avoid age legislation where there are no fixed retirement dates and employees can go "on and on". Secondly, because older people might well have more illnesses, government will fund sick pay, at the same rate as a full state pension.

Full time employees with more than 5 years' service will have the right to move onto grey contract hours once they reach the age of 60, with no loss of employment rights. This will ease them into retirement, while potentially creating a new job-share role to work alongside them. Controls will need to be put into place to ensure exploitation does not take place and that these roles are not driving out full-time employment. Public sector employers such as teaching, NHS and the police will be targeted to create a set proportion of grey roles.

Public service

We often hear that important public services are under-staffed. We should encourage people at the beginning and at the end of their time in full time work to help. This will be called National Service. This will not just be in the armed services; we will have national service roles in all of our public services. Society will expect people, sometime in their lives, to give back. Careers will be planned around this and employers will expect it. Employers will value younger people that have engaged in such work before commencing their chosen career. And through Community Credit, society will recognise and reward those people.

People like me are called the "baby boomer generation". This is the generation that my children think has messed up the world. We have been fortunate. We have not been asked to do national service. Most of us have never had to fight a war or move out of our comfort zone too much. We should be encouraged and helped to give something back. If we are lucky, we will live long. We will have plenty of time to do it.

The concept of Later Life National Service will fit well with the "grey contract" concept. Proper jobs, but with reduced hours, in public service roles. Many roles will be in the NHS, but the full gamut of public sector opportunities will be available, from teaching, policing, social services and local government, to front-line infantry. The young and the old will be the cavalry, riding in to give help, enthusiasm and experience where it is most needed.

Housing

Our housing problem will be solved through more intensive urban development, a more enlightened regional policy, and tax incentives for older people to downsize. Government can also help by building more high density publicly owned residences for working people and encouraging the building of publicly owned community and shared residences for elderly people. These properties could be financed and owned by the new National Money Purchase pension fund.

Every town, and every city, has within it badly used space, blighted areas and empty, ugly, and under-used property. Most of the homes in London and other cities are in buildings of only one or two floors. There is much opportunity for more vertical development and for more density of occupation. We don't need to solve the housing problem by finding more building-land in the greenbelt or in the countryside.

Domestic building conversion work that results in a new residence should be VAT-free. The income to the property owner from the sale should be Inheritance Tax and Capital Gains Tax exempt. Conversions will then be able to compete with new builds. Older people will be able to stay in their neighbourhood while at the same time helping to fund a healthy retirement. The large building corporations might not like it, but millions of small builders and retired people will.

A tax on the sale of domestic houses will be required to help repay our national debt. This will operate like VAT. Tax paid on the purchase of the property can be offset against the tax due on the sale. This tax will hit people that have lived in their homes for many years but did not pay tax on its purchase. This will be fair because, unlike younger buyers, people that have owned homes for many years did not pay stamp duty on them in the first place. To encourage empty-nesters to down-size early there will be an exemption for residents over 60 that have lived in their property for more than 10 years. But to exercise this exemption the property will need to be sold while they are still alive. If this does not happen, the tax will be collected from their estate on the sale of the property.

For there to be fairness in how public housing is allocated there should be a scoring system - both of housing and renters. People that have contributed to society should be given the best houses and be allowed to live in the best areas. For example, those people working in the caring professions should be given priority.

As we use urban land more intensively, then we will also need to create new public recreation areas and green spaces within it.

National standards for open space in urban areas will ensure that it will not just be the rich that have open space available to them. Each generation will leave new public spaces for the next – rather than continuingly leaning on our Victorian legacy.

In America, "condo living" - where services are supplied centrally to communities, is a popular method of retirement downsizing. Government can encourage the formation of such facilities – perhaps through standards and including some on-site NHS services. It could also build some public housing on this basis. Some retirement communities could even be in those warm countries where we have set up safe Overseas Development Areas. Ghana could become the UK's equivalent of Florida, but with fewer guns.

Protecting our environment

We must plan for a more local and regional structure of power generation and storage. Buildings converted to include unobtrusive solar generation, battery storage, and the ability to put electricity back into the grid. These features can be made compulsory in new building design.

Smaller modular nuclear power plant will play a part in the energy mix. The type of small nuclear reactors that are used to power submarines. Rolls Royce has experience of building these. The Russians and Chinese are developing small nuclear units that can be mass produced, floated to where they are needed, and then used floating on the surface, or moored beneath. Surrounding them in water provides emergency cooling that eliminates the danger of a catastrophic melt down. The UK is surrounded by water. This is an appropriate technology for us to be developing.

Industrial buildings with flat roofs should be used for solar generation. Anyone driving over the QE2 Bridge in London can see the potential. There are acres of unused flat roof over warehouse buildings. This ugly industrial landscape would be improved with the addition of solar power and wind turbines. The energy generated could be used locally. Many places like this exist.

We need a national clean-up plan. This will involve communities and landowners. One of the worst offenders is Railtrack. Alongside our railway tracks is the accumulated rubbish, and spare bits of kit, from many years. This all needs to be cleared away, together with the rubbish that accumulates alongside motorways and trunk-roads, particularly at junctions. Tagged and rewarded low risk prisoners could help - as could community offenders.

Throwing rubbish from cars will incur a single licence point penalty and a fine. The owner of the vehicle will be responsible. This type of behaviour can be captured on other drivers' dash-cams. Uploaded footage will be taken as evidence. Fixed cameras will also be set up at junctions to capture guilty parties.

Identity and personal data

The Aadhaar identity system in India has 99% of adults enrolled in it. The scheme has amassed the fingerprints and iris scans of over a billion people since 2010. With personal authorisation, any government body or private business can check whether the fingerprints or irises of a person match those recorded against a unique 12-digit identifying number recorded in a government database.

A system like this could revolutionise the provision of public services such as those provided by the NHS. A system like this could assist the police, the immigration services, and our security services. It will also make life considerably easier for ambulance services and for social services. The system could also be used to validate people joining dating sites and setting up social media accounts. The benefits to law abiding people are too great to ignore.

This system will also allow all public data about a person to be aggregated. This will include birth records, medical records, schooling, examination results, driving history, social points, and criminal records. This will be similar to a validated and private Facebook profile. The individual will own their own information, have access to it - and be able to decide who they allow to see certain parts of it.

In some instances, the authorities will be able to view a record. For instance, they will be able to use the system to identify those found sleeping rough. Social services will be able to trace back to find how and why these people have slipped through our network of social services. Each of these people will have a designated coach, and an action plan to get them back into stable accommodation with support. Charities will be able to use this information to help those in need. They can summarise a validated life history on a webpage outlining circumstances, life history, and needs. Cards can be printed

with links to a web page and to a na
way people can make an informed ch
know that their contributions will be
This system will also deter aggressive

These records already exist in vai
better for a system like this to be ope
place, rather than cobbled together cla
We can grapple with the privacy aspei
national debate. Ultimately, we as a
whether we go this way. A well worke(......... ....ul ve in the
manifesto of at least one of our political parties.

Infrastructure projects

The Brexit constitutional crisis has knocked national confidence and
cohesion. Any new incoming government will need to demonstrate
to the electorate, and the world, that it knows where we are going.
They will need a national plan that includes infrastructure
investment.

Infrastructure investment can be funded by Pension Bonds:
long-term debt funded by investment into the State Money Purchase
Pension Scheme. Government will guarantee Pension Bonds. The
assets financed will be income generating projects. With interest
rates currently low, this is a good time to invest in infrastructure.
These projects might be nationally important, or regionally
important. Each kingdom should bid for central funding for their
project ideas. Here are some suggestions.

A new London airport designated for flights to the East, at Cliffe, in
the Thames Estuary. This idea was previously christened Boris
Island, but would be better named The Eastern Airport. It will be a
sign to this rapidly developing part of the world that Britain is open
for business. This Eastern Airport will be helped by the planned new
river crossing linking the M2 south of the river with the M25 north
of the river. Freight traffic can use this to avoid the congested QE2
Bridge. We can combine the project with a tidal, solar, and wind park
to power the whole thing. Better still if it can also operate as the new
Thames barrage. The Eastern Airport could also be designed to
operate as a port for visiting cruise liners and for freight. Frequent
fast ferry links to Holland will reduce our reliance on the Channel

rench. Cruises to the Norwegian Fjords and to St
uld leave from here. Journeys into central London
by boat up the Thames. There will be links to the
ound and to the Channel Tunnel high speed railway line. Just
he river there is already access to the O2 concert venue, and to
remiership football at West Ham United. London Museums can
display exhibits here. There is also a world class conference centre at
the Excel Centre in Docklands. This will represent a great stop-over
experience in the same way as Dubai currently operates. As
happened in the development of Orlando in Florida, land could be
purchased and put aside for theme parks, retail, hotels and leisure –
some residential too. What better place to have the second Harry
Potter World, than in England? The National Pension Fund will
make a good profit on its investment.

In the West, an energy generating tidal barrage or tidal lagoons on
the Bristol Channel is crying out to be built. This could be combined
with clean, energy intensive, industries and water related leisure
activities. The area could become a hub for battery manufacture and
for the electric vehicle industry.

In Scotland, we have the promising MeyGen development of
turbines placed on the seabed. This is an exciting new clean energy
technology which has the potential for exports and significant
expansion.

We will need to build more storage devices to collect electricity
generated at times when it is not needed. Battery storage will play a
part, but large water pumping schemes will also be needed. These
are where water is pumped to a reservoir on the top of a hill when
surplus renewable energy is produced, e.g. at night, and then released
to power turbines when the power is required. Similar schemes use
heavy trains that climb mountains and then generate power on their
way down. We should create more of these facilities and make them
interesting and attractive. We might be able to re-open some deep
coal mineshafts and generate peak power by releasing very heavy
weights which have been winched to the surface during periods of
energy surplus. It would be great to use the relics of dirty energy to
help provide the clean energy of the future.

A National Grid for water is often discussed in those years that we have droughts. We now hear that projections indicate that water shortages in England are expected in the future. Let's build this national asset. If it can use our canals, it will also be a valuable tourist and leisure facility.

Our data infrastructure is as important as our physical infrastructure. Access to fast broadband must be available to all. Those that cannot access the internet will be increasingly affected by "digital poverty" as services and products move to an on-line only environment. The poor and the old are taken advantage of by suppliers that know they cannot shop around effectively.

The final part of our infrastructure to be improved is Government's process for buying things. The potential economies of scale from our huge public expenditure is squandered by fragmented buying decisions and negotiation. A Government sponsored version of Amazon (maybe set up with Amazon under a joint venture agreement) will require public bodies to use it to make all of their purchases. This will enable Government negotiated buying discounts – and produce detailed statistics of everything purchased with public money.

Technology

We should invest to develop world class tourism related technology. This will give Britain a lead in this important and growing market. Visitors to Britain will download their choice of Government approved "visit Britain" smartphone applications. These will function as the best tour guide that any tourist could wish to have. The specification for these applications will be to be multi-lingual, and capable of intelligent speech-based interaction – similar to Amazon's Alexa. People will be able to pay to break away from the virtual tour guide to have the services of a real online native concierge – fluent in their language. This person could help translate menus and give instructions to taxi drivers. They would be an exceptionally useful tour buddy.

Through headphones, the application will give information and guidance based on the location and interests of the user. The user will be able to focus their phone at a building or feature, and the application will explain its history. It will also help with safety, warning them when they are approaching high crime areas.

Pokémon Go has shown the attraction of augmented reality. This is where a fictional character or scene is overlaid onto a real life backdrop. This technology has huge potential in a country with such a rich historical legacy, and with such varied back-drops. The development of glasses that will take this experience away from the phone - and onto your sight-line - will open up massive opportunities for tourism. What tourist could not be excited by the prospect of looking out to sea in Norman's Bay in Sussex - and seeing William The Conqueror's fleet arriving in 1066. Of walking through Stratford Upon Avon - and seeing people everywhere in Tudor clothing. Of walking through Dickensian London at night - and seeing ghosts. The opportunities are huge.

Britain should set itself the target of full-scale visual augmentation of a historical city. That should be outside London. Somewhere like Cardiff, which has a fascinating history, but not the footfall of London. This city would become our shop-window for this technology. It will need to be given an industrial strength mobile internet system to make it work. This seed-investment will be like America's investment in the 1960s, to get a man on the moon. In our case, we won't be going to the moon - but through virtual reality we will be able to make people think that they are.

Policing

English devolution creates the opportunity to merge the 43 independent police forces in England and Wales into just ten forces. This will reflect the experience in Scotland, which has merged its eight regional police forces into a single national squad. This reorganisation will allow for better targeting by type of crime. A matrix structure will allow local forces to be focused on community crimes and prevention. These will be supported by national centres of excellence for each different type of crime. Crimes that are committed in cyber-space will be managed centrally, ideally in a centre of excellence for boffin plods, similar to GCHQ. This will give each type of crime sufficient expert attention. For example, mobile phone theft is endemic. With a more coherent approach to working with re-sellers, manufacturers and service providers, it can be stamped out. Specialist units, for example to tackle fraud, will improve accountability and competence, and provide interesting career paths.

Petty crime must also be taken seriously. The reporting of these types of post-crime incident can be made more efficient by use of national telephone lines and the internet. The car insurance industry has centralised and mechanised their claims reporting process through "FNOL" units, which stands for First Notification of Loss. The police could replicate this, using internet reporting and call centres. The police and the public also need some better ways to deal with property offenders, unruly and often drunken or drugged people, and armed criminals and terrorist. This will involve a review of the trespass laws, more low-level sanctions, and better physical protection.

Where youngsters or drunks behave badly towards the police, the ability to quickly identify them is important. Biometric identity systems will be a huge deterrent. The ability to issue low level sanctions and fines, without leaving a criminal record, will also be very helpful. For example, police could register negative social points. They could also confiscate mobile phones or trainers, temporarily replacing smartphones with a basic model, and trainers with yellow slippers of shame.

During riots the police need a way to identify masked offenders. Paint ball guns will do this. A paint ball can be designed to leave a unique and indelible mark on clothing and skin. Gun sights can include cameras which record the illegal activity, e.g. throwing missiles at the police, and register each shot against a unique paintball DNA. The paint and the linked picture will provide identity and evidence. These guns will also be a deterrent, because being hit with a paintball is painful.

Most of our police should be armed. At Borough Market three terrorists with knives were tackled by a policeman with a truncheon. That is not right. A light-weight small-bore handgun, with limited ammunition, will give our community police a fighting chance of holding up and injuring terrorists and gangsters. A gunshot also puts the population on alert. Each police gun would incorporate a GPS monitor and a sim card. If it was fired or stolen, it would send a distress signal with the gun's precise location. This will allow police ninjas to make their way to the scene.

The BBC

The BBC is one of the best recognised and trusted brands in the world. It is a huge asset to the UK. But it has lost its mojo. In a world with so much media choice and polarised opinions, it appears bloated, old fashioned and directionless. It is also expensive, with an out of date funding model. It needs to reinvent itself. The licence fee is a regressive and unfair tax. It is levied at the same rate no matter how much of the BBC product is consumed. Most people now get much of their media content from other sources, for example Netflix. A new funding model is needed. Self-funding of the BBC can be achieved through advertising, sharpening its offering and by launching a global internet-based subscription channel based on the Netflix model. The BBC owns huge amounts of historical content that it can make available.

BBC's TV channels need to be re-ordered along commercial lines. BBC1 stays as it is - a general entertainment channel. We then have channels for News, Sport, Education, Comedy and Music. BBC Sport should focus on British sport that would otherwise not get an airing, and on youth sport and local events. New style "home internationals" for sports would be based around the Nine English Kingdoms and Scotland, Wales and Northern Ireland. A league of twelve. Games in these competitions would be televised on the BBC, with advertisements to help fund these leagues. For example, in football, to help young domestic players, we can set up a "Twelve Kingdoms" televised Under-21 league. The parallel is American college football, which is wildly popular. These leagues will allow UK talent and managers to develop and will foster "kingdom identity", and community spirit. There will be both men's and ladies' leagues, so most weeks a game will be on TV.

The subscription-based streaming model is already under construction. Hopefully, it will have regionalised and foreign language versions and include a channel focused on helping people to learn English. It must be non-political and non-judgemental, a revenue generating tool, and a show case for British talent, the English language, and the British way of life. The other huge asset is the BBC website. This is already doing very well. It's free to use model has allowed it to develop along similar lines to Facebook. This is one of the few areas where Britain owns an internet champion.

8

EUROPE

Constitutions may be undermined from without as well as from within. This happens when they are confronted by a constitution of an opposite type, which either is their close neighbour or is powerful even if distant. It happened in the days of the Athenian and Spartan empires. The Athenians everywhere put down oligarchies; the Spartans, in turn, suppressed democracies.

Aristotle, Politics

Brexit has become the background to our lives. It looks as though the European issue will be with us for some time to come. These events are a supreme example of poor policy decision making, poor execution, and a lack of planning and competence in government. The mechanics of leaving and the type of relationship we should ask for were not worked through. Following the vote, the weaknesses of our party structures and political system are there for all to see.

The conduct of the EU referendum demonstrated the desirability of having a democratic House of Lords to authorise trusted facts and statistics in advance of elections or referendums. In business, major decisions are made with the help of cost-benefit analysis. Non-financial costs and benefits can be argued by both sides. Forecasts for financial costs and benefits will be examined and debated by experts. But existing and historical statistics, including EU costs and benefits, should be factual. It will help our democracy if a "fact book" can be produced by the House of Lords and published in advance of every election or referendum.

This book was not intended to be about our relationship with the EU, or with our Europe neighbours. There are so many other things we need to focus upon domestically. But because people's views on these issues have become so politically charged, a book like this cannot be written today without the author explaining their position on the European question.

A formative experience

In my biography, in the appendix, I explain a little about my short time working within the RBS Group. Up until the time that my company was purchased by Fred Goodwin's RBS, I had been fortunate in that I was either on the board that was making the decisions, or I was able to make representations to sensible and receptive people on the board above. That wasn't the case under RBS. I was expected to carry out decisions made elsewhere, and if I didn't agree with those decisions, there was nothing much I could do about it. That's why I decided to leave.

This experience came back to me when later on in my career, in 2011, insurance pricing was brought to the EU's attention as an example of illegal gender discrimination. The insurance industry was caught wrong-footed by this. We couldn't believe that such a strong rating factor was at risk of being taken away. The driving performance of the sexes is different. Young men, fuelled by testosterone and an inflated view of their abilities, are 4 times more likely to have an accident as young women. I helped the Association of British Insurers to lobby for this change not to happen, meeting with MPs. Little good it did us. We had to change our systems and pricing so that we charged the same for 17-year-old men as we did for 17-year-old women. Younger women now pay more than they should. Young men now pay less, cross-subsidised by their safer female counterparts.

This policy change was wrong, resulting in more dangerous young male drivers on the road. But the lasting impact on me was the sense of powerlessness from our MPs. They had become accustomed to accepting that Head Office told them what to do - and they could do nothing about it. They were using the EU to escape their accountability for bad laws.

The EU referendum

When the EU referendum negotiations began, my hope and expectation was that David Cameron would obtain significant concessions. The output of his renegotiation was important. The EU was sucking more and more power to the centre. It was becoming increasingly meddlesome in domestic policy. Our national democracy was being gradually picked apart and weakened by the EU's march towards commonality and a rule based bureaucratic central power. My preference was reform rather than departure. EU reform that would respect our position outside of the Euro block. Cameron's strategy for achieving this reform was flawed in both its planning and execution. To try so publicly to get change, to fail so obviously, and for this to then be "put to bed" by a positive referendum result would put us in a very weak position from which to push for change. In these circumstances, a Remain vote would give the EU a mandate from the UK not to change, to continue as they were.

During the campaign the negative and threatening approach of the Remain argument was flawed and annoying. Anyone with a sense of British history or patriotism would not be able to accept that we could not survive on our own. We are not that weak. And if we had somehow become so, it must be due to our creeping loss of independence to the EU. Despite many positive feelings towards the EU, I found myself a reluctant Leaver. My hope was that we could use a Leave vote to engineer a new and a better relationship with the EU. It has been shocking and disappointing to see how poorly we have gone about this. It has been embarrassing. It has been damaging to our national reputation. It has damaged each of our political parties. It has damaged the way we think about our MPs.

German influence in the EU

The formation of the Euro block has changed the dynamics of power in the EU. The Euro block is calling the shots in the EU. The country calling the shots in the Euro block is Germany. The way this German influence works is explained in Berlin Rules: Europe and the German Way, written by Paul Lever, former British ambassador to Germany from 1997 to 2003. As Lever notes, "Britain felt directly the reality of German power in the EU during David Cameron's attempt to renegotiate the terms of its membership. It was a chastening experience. In the end he had to settle for some minor change to social security entitlements. It was widely, and rightly, seen as a defeat."

Bagehot remarked on the Germanic way of doing things, "Just now the triumph of the Prussians – the bureaucratic people, as is believed, par excellence – has excited a kind of admiration for bureaucracy." He saw bureaucratic government as the most unimproving and shallow of Governments. "The functionaries are not there for the benefit of the people, but the people for the benefit of the functionaries. A bureaucracy is sure to think that its duty is to augment official powers, official business, or official members, rather than to leave free the energies of mankind."

Bureaucratic governments generate rules. English people do not like too many rules. Rules constrain our freedom and our creativity. We put up with them if we see sense in them, but we feel within our rights to ignore stupid ones, or to push back. Bagehot celebrated this national character trait, "The natural impulse of the English people is to resist authority. Our freedom is the result of centuries of resistance, more or less legal, or more or less illegal, more or less audacious, or more or less timid, to the executive government."

Deal, no deal, second referendum

We must honour the referendum result and leave the EU, but that should be through a deal with a negotiated withdrawal. It will take time to unpick the areas of EU control. Once the heat is off, we might find that we can agree accommodating arrangements. We need time to explore what a hard Brexit with separate trading agreements would look like. Time to consider what the people of Northern Ireland think is best for it.

An agreed withdrawal process will also give the EU time to reflect on the reasons for our people's rejection of them. Time to consider a different form of membership for the UK. Some EU introspection and reform could keep one of their largest members in the tent. A progressive EU should prove that it can listen - and that it can change. In the next few years the EU will see a new parliament, a new president, and a new German Chancellor. This could help this process to happen.

The concept of a second vote that would have the potential to overturn the first vote is dangerous, divisive and undemocratic. The

British people have already voted on our previous membership arrangements. They should not be asked to do so again. How can they trust Parliament to enact any new referendum when the last vote was not honoured? We need to leave, and then should only be asked to vote again if a new form of EU membership is offered that is genuinely different, one that deals with the issues arising from our previous membership, identified in the next section. A new form of membership like this could be put to the country, maybe with the alternative being a fully worked out form of hard Brexit. But this time the details of both options need to be fully worked out in advance – and MPs fully committed to implementing the decided outcome.

Eight messages to the EU from the British people

We failed to agree on a coherent and concise message to the EU for the reasons for the British Brexit vote. That was a huge error. We failed to "pick the bones" from the Leave vote. Branding Leavers as stupid, racist and xenophobic was untrue and an error of judgement. We let the EU off the hook. They did not need to respond to clearly articulated and reasonable objections to their model, and to their rule. It is not too late to agree on clear messages to the EU. Eight messages that explain the vote in the context of a reaction to an EU that wasn't prepared to listen or to change.

1.   Social inequality: the free movement of labour has depressed the wages of working-class British residents. It restricts job opportunities for unskilled nationals. The open nature of the British service economy, and the widespread use in the EU of English as a second language, means that working-class Europeans can easily work in England. But free movement does not work nearly so well in the other direction. There are not many working-class British that have the language skills – or the local permits - to work in Europe, assuming that those jobs are available in the first place.

2.   Infrastructure strain: the free movement of people together with Britain's generous welfare benefits and open labour markets attracts large numbers of people from lower wage and lower opportunity areas of the EU. This puts strain on our infrastructure and our public services and reduces the quality of life in some of the most densely populated areas of Europe.

3. Community strain: Britain is an open and diverse economy. It welcomes newcomers. But in some areas the actual and potential numbers of new migrants puts this cohesion under pressure. People and places are not getting enough help to adapt.

4. Border control: The breakdown of immigration controls in some parts of the EU is a concern. Camps of people willing to risk their lives to get out of France and into Britain strengthens the impression of an island country under siege.

5. Influence: The Euro block is becoming more integrated and starting to pursue its own agenda. UK influence is reducing, as seen by the appointment of Juncker despite strong opposition from the UK. Further integration will be necessary for the Euro block which will see us get further away from the core decision-making group.

6. Centralisation of power: European courts interfere too much in UK decision making. There is a feeling that UK democracy and accountability is being weakened by powers moving to EU bureaucrats. British people value freedom, sovereignty and their democracy above all things. They do not want to lose these in a move to become a European super-state.

7. Lack of accountability: UK politicians have been vilified for profligate expense claims. The country has been experiencing austerity. There is a sense that there is poor financial control in the EU, with some dubious practices - and an EU budget that is not under control.

8. Lack of flexibility: The vote was very close. British people love many things about the EU. The UK has helped to build it into what it is today. It will be weaker without us. There is a huge sadness, and a reluctance to leave. Why is it that the EU is so rigid and unbending that they can't come back with a way to address our concerns and to keep us in? Why can't it consider change? These things do not reflect well on the EU institution or its leaders.

We have the potential to take our eight key messages directly to EU voters through PR. Macron took this route with his open letter to European newspapers.

EU negotiations

Our approach should always have been to hope for peace, but to prepare for war. Not a war that involves fighting, but a war that involves dealing with a negotiating party that is prepared to play hard ball to get what it wants. A negotiating party that is not attempting to find a win-win solution, but that want a win-lose solution. In EU terms, that is an attempt to inflict a "punishment Brexit" to dissuade other members from following our path.

Under Theresa May our tactics were naïve and transparent. We showed ourselves to be weak, divided, and awkward. We were arrogant, upset our natural allies, overestimated our strengths, underestimated the strengths of the other side, and were soundly trounced in the opening battles. All failings that will be familiar to any student of British warfare over the ages. We needed to regroup, to rethink our approach, and to recruit some better generals.

The ideal objective should be some form of soft Brexit, with the door open to return at a later stage once the EU has evolved and matured, and also with an option to move in the other direction, to a harder form of Brexit. That respects the referendum result, while also allowing the EU and the British people then to get closer together, or further apart, depending on circumstances and the changing politics of the EU and the UK.

Chess players make good negotiators because they are constantly looking at the game, both from their own position, but also from the position of their opponent. If I make this move, how will they counter? What attacking plays could I or they make? We also need psychological profiling of the people that are negotiating from our side, and from theirs. How do we push the right buttons, how will our and their people react when under stress? There is an art and a science to negotiations, and our amateur approach under Theresa May was embarrassing.

The EU have played their cards skilfully. Thankfully, it seems that we have now entered the game. We have some strong cards.

A democratic mandate. In the short term we will be damaged economically from our exit. That was made clear during the campaign. But we still voted to leave. That demonstrates an admirable part of the British character. We will make self-sacrifices when we feel our freedom is at stake. Our Government has a democratic mandate for our withdrawal from the EU. They also have a democratic mandate for incurring some pain on the way out. But the EU does not have a mandate to punish its people in higher import taxes and lower growth. It has no democratic mandate to pursue a punishment Brexit.

Trade. The EU exports huge amounts more to us than we export to them. These numbers should be published and advertised, showing individual European country trade balances - and some individual company figures, e.g. BMW, VW and Mercedes. We can start to prepare a policy response should the EU chose to apply taxes to our exports to them - supporting British made goods and encouraging import substitution. We will bring back country of origin labelling. Websites will help consumers and companies source UK made goods.

Global influence. The EU will be reduced by our departure. The trading block will be smaller and our contributions to the EU budget will be lost. The EU will have less global influence.

Disengagement. A Brexit that ends in rancour, sanctions, fines and Britain feeling victimised and hard done by will be a dangerous victory for the EU to win. Germany's national mood after World War One is a warning for what can happen when a nation feels humiliated and victimised. Britain might disengage with the EU and find new friends in other parts of the world. It might adopt a different business model. That could be untrammelled capitalism, or socialism, depending on the wishes of the British people. It will be uncomfortable for the EU to have such a place so close to them.

Public relations

So far, the EU has triumphed at PR, framing the UK's negotiations as chaotic, unstructured, rude and arrogant. The reason for our dislike of the free movement of people principle has not been explained or understood. Our own media has been a great help to them. We need to up our game on PR.

The UK should position itself as the champion of democracy and for those losing out from globalisation. The messages from Brexit are also coming from the people in other parts of the EU, but the EU's elite class - and the EU's bureaucrats – they're not listening. Any trade sanctions that arise that were not there before will hurt EU consumers and workers. Tariffs are just another form of taxation. It will be the EU's consumers that pay the price of a hard Brexit, also the workers in those industries that export to us.

The tensions in the Euro area will need to be resolved by a closer political union of those that are in it. This will require transfer payments to outlying areas. The EU needs to resolve this issue so that the UK can determine what any future membership will look like. Pressure on the EU's external borders will increase. We will work with the EU to help them to develop a coherent and agreed policy response. It is a concern to us that they have not been able to do this up to now. It is in our mutual interests to continue to work closely together on security and technological developments and in balancing the influence of China, Russia and the USA. Pushing the UK away will force us to get closer to other global power blocks.

The EU's greatest fear in negotiation is that we seek to marginalise their bureaucrats by taking our arguments directly to member governments. That we seek to divide them. So, of course, that is exactly what we should do. It is not in the interests of most EU nations to lose our counter to French and German self interest in EU policy making. Our defence capability will also be valuable in years to come. And low wage migrants making it into the EU will no longer be able to come to Britain, so they will be heading in greater numbers to other EU countries. We need to identify and nurture our key allies inside the camp. We also need to build stronger links with those European countries that are outside the EU, in particular, Norway and Switzerland.

UK policy changes

One of the valid themes from Remainers was that the UK's problems with the EU were largely self-inflicted through poor policy choices and policy development. We need to work this through. Any future move to re-join the EU needs to identify and promote the policy changes that will solve these problems. If we wanted to construct a tax and benefits system that attracted low-skilled EU workers to move here to compete with UK workers, we couldn't have done much better than the one we had in place. Not only do we have a very high threshold before we tax low wage workers, we also subsidise them with tax credits.

We need to improve our domestic border controls so that we know that everyone is here legally. Biometric identity cards and a national payroll system will reduce the pull factor for illegal immigrants. The EU will also benefit from a rule that migrants that have been granted residency or asylum in one EU country will need to reside for some time in that country before they obtain the right to move to another.

The way EU laws are applied needs consideration. For many national democrats, it is an affront that EU courts should have more power than the courts of Sovereign countries. In particular, in the interpretation of Human Rights laws. There is a case for these to be framed by each country within the EU, provided that divergence from the norm has a clear domestic democratic mandate. In more general terms, the EU should be considering political and structural reform itself. Those that believe in the UK's future within the EU weaken their case when they accept that the decision-making and democratic processes within the EU make reform of its institutions or its rules impossible.

9

CHANGING THE GAME

There was a practical wisdom in our ancestors, which induced them to alter and vary the form of our institutions as they went on: to suit them to the circumstances of the time, and reform them according to the dictates of experience. They never ceased to work upon our frame of government, as a sculptor fashions the model of a favourite statue.

Lord John Russell, principal architect of the Great Reform Act of 1832

This has been a tumultuous time for British politics. In a short period, we have had two, and probably soon three, general elections and two referendums, one on Scottish independence and one on EU membership. The EU referendum result has put huge strain on our political system. It has changed how each of us thinks about our political allegiances. These interesting times are difficult to live through, but interesting times in British politics are nothing new. Over the last thousand years British political institutions have evolved through a series of shocks to the system.

Magna Carta in 1215 began the process of setting up of a framework of laws to control our leaders, then represented by the king. David Starkey's book, Magna Carta, explains how at Runnymede the unpopular King John, (the king that is represented by a lion in Disney's Robin Hood film), who had lost our Continental inheritance, was forced by a coalition of 25 powerful barons to limit his powers. This was done by making him sign a charter of rights. The Chronicle of Melrose Abbey recorded this event: "A new state of things has begun in England; such a strange affair as has never been heard; for the body wished to rule the head, and the people desired to be masters over the king."

The struggle to reform parliament

By the beginning of the nineteenth century power had largely been removed from the monarchy and was in the hands of Parliament. Members of Parliament were generally the aristocracy and the gentry, standing for boroughs that hugely varied in size. Only a small number of property-owning men were allowed to vote, and no women at all. Most of this century, a time when Britain rose to be the wealthiest and most powerful nation in the world, was accompanied by a background of popular struggle for political change. These demands were continually resisted by established power, but eventually resulted in fundamental reforms to our political system. The Victorians were huge game changers, although in those days they called it reform.

The first fight was for universal male suffrage – for every man to be able to vote. This process began with the Great Reform Act of 1832. It continued with the Second Reform Act of 1867. Organised demands for women's suffrage started to take shape at about this time. It took three more reform acts, in 1884, 1918, and 1928, before universal suffrage was achieved, and everyone could vote. This was achieved with the 1928 Equal Franchise Act. At this stage the franchise applied to all those over 21. This was extended to those over 18 years old in 1966.

All of these changes were achieved as a result of public pressure. Power was wrestled away from the monarchy, the aristocracy, and finally, in 1928, from men. Some would consider that particular part of reform to still be a work in progress. As said by Ernest Jones, one of the Reform League's most charismatic public speakers; "liberty was never yet given as a present to a nation. It was always won by the people themselves."

The next two sections explain the use of petitions in the nineteenth century and the development of the Chartist movement. They draw upon the House of Common's website, Parliament.uk.

The use of petitions

In the nineteenth century people used their Members of Parliament to raise their problems and concerns with those powerful enough to make changes. The most common way to influence Parliament was to present MPs with petitions. They often demanded changes in the law and could be presented by individuals, whole communities or organised groups.

Demands for change covered subjects such as the abolition of slavery, and parliamentary reform. The number of petitions, and the number of petitioners, grew rapidly from the end of the 18th century. In 1839 13,657 public petitions were presented on more than 90 different subjects with a total of over 4.5 million signatures.

In 1843, issues including repeal of the Corn Laws and support for and opposition to the Factories Bill led to a peak of 6,135,050 signatories on petitions to the House of Commons in that year. In 1893/4 a record 33,742 separate petitions were received, on a wide variety of issues including the established Church in Wales, the government of Ireland and control of liquor traffic.

The Chartist movement

The Chartist movement was the first mass movement driven by the working classes. It grew following the failure of the 1832 Reform Act to extend the vote beyond those owning property. In 1838 a People's Charter was drawn up for the London Working Men's Association (LWMA) by William Lovett and Francis Place, two self-educated radicals, in consultation with other members of LWMA.

The Charter had six demands. That all men should have the vote. That voting should take place by secret ballot. That Parliamentary elections should take place every year, not once every five years. That constituencies should be of equal size. That Members of Parliament should be paid, and that the property qualification for becoming a Member of Parliament should be abolished

In 1839, the Chartists' petition was presented to the House of Commons with over 1.25 million signatures. It was rejected by Parliament. This provoked unrest which was crushed by the authorities. A second petition was presented in 1842, signed by over three million people but again it was rejected, and further unrest and arrests followed.

In 1848 a third and final petition was presented. A mass meeting on Kennington Common in South London was organised by the Chartist movement leaders. The most influential leader was Fergus O'Connor, editor of 'The Northern Star', a weekly newspaper that promoted the Chartist cause. The authorities feared disruption and military forces were on standby to deal with any unrest. This petition was also rejected but the anticipated unrest did not happen.

Despite the Chartist leaders' attempts to keep the movement alive, within a few years it was no longer a driving force for reform. However, the Chartists' legacy was strong. By the 1850s Members of Parliament accepted that further reform was inevitable. Further Reform Acts were passed in 1867 and 1884. By 1918, five of the Chartists' six demands had been achieved - only the stipulation that parliamentary elections be held every year was unfulfilled.

Political unions

The principle of people lobbying politicians for change is nothing new. The organisation described in Chapter three is only new in its use of modern technology. The principle of an extra-parliamentary organisations formed to promote and campaign for change was established some 189 years ago by those pushing for parliamentary reform. These organisations were locally based and were called "political unions". The first political union was founded in Birmingham in January 1830. By 1832 there were more than one hundred political unions in towns across the United Kingdom. David Cannadine, in his book about the period, notes that these organisations included disaffected Tories and Whigs pressing determinedly for parliamentary reform. They encompassed a wide range of social backgrounds and an equally broad spectrum of political opinion. They harnessed the intensifying mood of popular discontent and public disenchantment of that time. In December 1830 Joseph Parkes of the Birmingham political union wrote to Francis Place of the London Political Union. "There are times when the Government should be told plainly what the people demand and will have... Thank God we are now dependent on no party."

Developing pressure for political change

Modern Britons have lost their hunger for political reform. There is a feeling that our political institutions are unchanging. There is a feeling that the job of reform is done. Modern reformers need to find their mojo. They need to tap into the reforming zeal possessed by their nineteenth century ancestors. The vote we are given is ineffective if the system does not allow political parties to emerge that reflect our views. It is ineffective if we live in a constituency dominated by one party. It is ineffective if the MPs it produces do not adequately reflect our views, or the views of the nation.

The frustrations and anger of people following the political crisis generated by the EU referendum result has "woken" people to the problems in our system. Problems which have caused us to vote for politicians who do not represent our views. Problems which have allowed political parties to put their own interests ahead of the interests of the country.

The Chartists demonstrated the value of building a common framework for a campaign for political change, for reform. But to be successful, this cause must be owned by the people. In the twenty first century this will require *Modern Political Unions*. These will be organisations that draw upon the power of new technology - and the reforming energy of the nineteenth century.

The campaigns by Remainers and Brexiteers have started this process, binding people behind ideas rather than parties. Once the Brexit bubble has been burst, this energy, from both sides, needs to swing behind a concerted push to improve the system. A system that allowed our politicians to create a situation that put well-meaning groups of British people, from both sides of the debate, so implacably against each other.

A new charter for political change

The Chartists looked back to 1215 and the concept of a charter demanding a list of political demands. Unlike the Magna Carta, which was long, and drawn up by barons, Chartists focused on just six simple demands. These could be easily explained to people. Chartism was a populist movement, unlike the Magna Carta, which was more elitist, driven by the aristocracy.

The changes we need can also be summarised into six themes. These can form the foundations of a popular movement.

1. Voters need better information at elections
2. English regions need devolved power from Westminster
3. Young people need greater electoral power
4. Voters want to vote separately on party and candidate
5. The House of Lords needs to become democratic
6. Our political system needs to change - from top to bottom

These themes can be built into six specific demands in a new Charter. The working assumption is that it be called *The Game Changer's Charter.* This will call for six specific reforms.

1. A prescribed format and timetable for election manifestos
2. English devolution to The Nine Kingdoms of England
3. A reduction of the voting age to 16
4. The Additional List voting system
5. A democratic and reformed House of Lords
6. Pre-agreed retirement dates for our next three kings

The last demand is a populist measure to represent more business-like government and to make the point that all aspects of our system need to be reviewed. If we are to review the workings of Government, to make them more efficient and accountable, then this process should start with a good example at the top. The implementation of retirement dates will open up a debate about the tasks we expect a modern head of state to perform. This debate will then cascade down to all levels of government.

Each of these headline proposals will need detailed policies behind them. That is where a policy production website will play its part. Detailed polices will be fleshed out and publicly available for inspection and comment. These proposals can be worked up so that there is ready-to-go legislation behind them. This can then be enacted by a vote of "Game Changing" MPs in Parliament.

An internet-based lobby system will be a super-efficient version of the chartists' petitions. Each MP will know exactly how many of their constituencies are in favour of the charter. But crucially, unlike the original Chartists, these people already have the vote. They will use it to get reform supportive candidates elected.

Building political support

The two parties that benefit most from leaving our political system as it is are the Conservative Party and the Labour Party. Both parties have a strong vested interest to resist change. Both parties have experienced power under our first-past-the post system. Both parties have a broadly-based membership encompassing a wide selection of political views. But this situation is breaking down. The Conservatives are split over Europe and their different visions for a post Brexit UK. Labour are split over their leader's rejection of "New Labour" and his support for a more extreme form of socialism. Both parties look old fashioned and ill prepared to grapple with the problems and aspirations of ordinary people. To get better choices, political parties which are more competent and more responsive to the concerns of the electorate, the system needs to change. A changed system will allow more diverse choices and for more distinctive and innovative policy proposals.

An organisation set up to back the Charter can help by working with progressive and reforming MPs within each of the parties to agree a common position on constitutional change. There will be some unlikely bedfellows, but the potential prize of a more diverse and responsive political system is huge. If people from different parties can have the self-discipline to speak with one voice on this one issue - constitutional change – the impact on the public could be immense.

Governance

An agenda for political reform may sound dull to some, but to others it will sound radically progressive. It has the potential to change the way that politics happens in the United Kingdom. It will disrupt power structures. A popular movement that promotes and owns this agenda will need governance and leadership. It will need a high-profile board containing a cross section of political views and experience. The board will need some high-profile politicians, but also people that have not worked in politics, and people to represent the regions. It will need diversity. Finally, the board will need a strong chair. This organisation will also need good relations with the UK's regulator of political activity, The Electoral Commission. This independent body will be an important stakeholder in this activity.

No individual political party can be trusted to change the rules of the political game. These changes need to come from pressure from outside, from those with no vested interest in the outcome.

An alliance for change

The Brexit process has shown how separate groups within political parties can work together. To be successful, the Charter will need to be supported by groups of *"Game Changers"* within both Labour and the Conservatives. One or both of these parties might come around to supporting elements of it, or perhaps all of it, although that might be seen as turkeys voting for Christmas.

Outside these two parties, all the remaining parties can be expected to be natural supporters. The changes proposed will give them a better chance at elections and for their policies to shine. Hopefully, they can work together to help shape a common agenda and the detailed policies and legislation required to enact it.

Tactical voting – a scenario

Political unions with databases of supporters have the potential to put their support behind candidates in each constituency. If Brexit is not concluded before the next election, we can expect to see Remain political unions promoting the most likely Remain candidates, and Leave political unions doing the reverse. This could result in a hung parliament, and a very angry and frustrated electorate. Our electoral process will have produced another unsatisfactory result. A carefully worked out electoral reform agenda might then be welcomed. A coalition of Game Changers could emerge and promote the changes needed to have the next election using a better system.

This scenario would be hugely challenging for vested interests. But it would be hugely fertile in helping to re-shape political parties, re-energise British democracy - and in helping to set a new direction for the country.

The need for political realignment

As splits in each of the major parties have emerged, it has become apparent that a political realignment and some new choices are required. The behaviour and limitations of our existing political parties is not only annoying the public, it is annoying a good proportion of their own MPs and party members. Change is in the air, and how we need it. Commentators from across the political spectrum have been demanding change, but there is a lack of optimism that meaningful political change can be achieved. It seems as though there is no safe mechanism to make this happen. Our political system is stuck in a groove.

The proposals in this book are designed to allow our system to move on. Each party could significantly mature and evolve under a system that allowed people to choose a party that most reflected their political outlook, as well as a candidate most reflective of our individual values. Each of us can then safely choose the candidate most able to represent our views and our local constituency.

Even in a system like this, it is unlikely that our own individual political philosophies will be replicated in any one party. But when parties are forced to work together it might be possible to get much of what we want. The Conservative and Liberal Democrat coalition was a good example of how parties with different philosophies can work together for the common good – cherry picking and sense checking each other's policies.

How our political parties might evolve

This section looks at how each of our parties might develop under a new electoral system.

The Scottish Nationalists' breed of socialism appeals to many in the Labour party. As a more broadly based *"Nationalist"* party, they could champion devolution and the strengthening of local communities in all parts of the UK, including England. They could represent another potential home for those in the Labour party who are not comfortable with Jeremy Corbyn. English nationalism doesn't come with a belief that England needs to leave the UK. English nationalists believe that England can be the best it can be as part of the UK. Scottish Nationalists might eventually evolve and take that approach too. As Nationalists they can champion devolution in the UK in all its forms, including English devolution.

English regions need a champion against the centralising tendencies of the Conservative and Labour parties. They will keep power in Westminster if they can. A repositioned Nationalist Party, for all the regions, could have great influence in helping to make the United Kingdoms a union of equals, a union that the Scottish would not want to leave.

Part of their policy promise will be to work on an "Article 50" type process for any part of the UK to leave and become independent. If the Union is working well, then no part of the Union would ever want to trigger it. The current EU exit negotiations show the complexity of exiting a Union. Any voter for independence should know the process, the problems, and the size of the exit bill, well in advance of any vote. The SNP's Brexit message that "people didn't vote to be poorer" can then be put to the test in the context of leaving a highly successful union that is over 300 years old.

Scotland joining the EU may not be simple. There will be the border issue that we have seen caused so much trouble in Ireland. There may also be Spain in the way. The Scottish people will have observed how Catalonia was treated by Spain during its attempt at independence. Its leaders were locked up for insurrection. The EU looked the other way. And maybe Nicola Sturgeon hasn't noticed, but she's running one of those "nationalist" parties that EU bureaucrats talk about with such derision. Better to belong to a union that, despite its flaws, is democratic. A union where you have influence. A union that respects your right to self-determination.

The Liberal Democrats should be the party promoting freedom, promoting democracy, promoting English devolution. They should be seeking to take apart the apparatus of inherited power and privilege. From the Liberal Democrats we expect new ideas for a progressive policy towards engagement with the EU, and distinctive policies for the UK itself. Unfortunately, their current position on Brexit has alienated over half of their potential voters and tarnished their democratic credentials. To correct this, they will need to accept that the British people have rejected the EU as it is and come up with a vision for a changed EU, and a changed UK/EU relationship. Currently, they look like one of those despised populist parties - but their populism is of the pro-EU kind.

The Green Party is focused on the health of the planet as a whole. They take a Globalist outlook. They have many good policies and an excellent website listing these, but many of their wider political views and polices alienate green sympathetic voters. In particular, their views on migration and borders and aspects of their economic policy. In Europe, Green parties work effectively in coalitions. Under an Additional List voting system, environmentally concerned voters can back Green candidates with strong environmental credentials, while at the same time backing a party that has a more traditional economic policy.

UKIP did very badly at the 2017 general election. The Conservatives stole their Brexit fur coat. Voters saw that they had absolutely nothing on underneath - apart from a few offensive tattoos. If they have a future beyond campaigning on Europe, it will be to become a right-wing English nationalist party. It will be ironic if they do this while right-wing nationalism is growing in the EU.

Change UK MPs showed courage to break away from Labour and the Conservatives. But the Liberal Democrat Party has proved to be more attractive to pro-EU supporters, and most of their founding MPs have deserted them. Electoral reform would have given them a greater chance to establish themselves.

The Labour Party did unexpectedly well in the 2017 election. People liked that they had principles and policies which flowed from them. They liked that they listened, and that they answered questions directly. They liked that they gave their membership power. They liked that they engaged with younger people. But they didn't trust them to run the country. If today's Labour party are to get into power, they need to bridge a gap in trust with explicit and well worked out policies. There can be no vague ideas, no expansion of debt funded spending. If more money is required, then the tax implications need to be fully explained. A strengthened and democratic House of Lords will help improve Labour's credibility, by putting in place controls to guard against an irresponsible post-election spending spree using borrowed money.

Labour will continue to redefine its socialist values for the new age. It has identified the young as a group that have been disadvantaged by the accumulation of wealth and power by older generations. It will be the party of higher taxes, greater redistribution, increased regulation, with a larger role for the state in social care. It will look more attractive if it can modernise itself, rethinking how public services can be improved and become more efficient.

Labour's main challenge will be to reconcile its metropolitan focus on identity politics, globalism, and individual rights, with its traditional working-class support. A Donald Trump inspired plain-speaking patriotic and populist party could capture its hinterland, which feels forgotten. It will be difficult for Labour to court both "the deplorables" and the liberal intelligentsia.

The Conservative Party has found the Brexit negotiations to be traumatic. It is not natural for a party that is associated with stability and conservatism to have to enact such a radical policy. Three distinctive factions have emerged. "Hard Brexiteers" who are keen to leave the EU and to adopt a free trading and free market approach. "Soft Brexiters" who accept that we will leave the EU, even though they may not have wanted that to happen and hope for an eventual rapprochement which might involve joining again. Finally, "Stubborn Remainers" that did not accept the Brexit vote and have tried to resist it, pushing for a second referendum. Currently, it looks as though the Stubborn Remainers have been marginalised.

In a system with more political choice, and more credible alternatives, the Conservatives will need to develop a more distinctive set of policies and values. Just being better than Labour should not be enough to earn our votes. They will also need to decide if they will embrace UK political reform. English devolution is unlikely to sit comfortably with them. They can also be expected to resist a reduction of the voting age given their poor reputation with young people. But Brexiteers within the party might find a re-energising of our domestic political system difficult to resist. This will be a tangible outcome of returning powers to the UK from the EU.

A new political party

This leaves a gap in the political market, explained by Rod Liddle of the Times. "Those who live outside London and dislike identity politics, political correctness and untrammelled immigration, who support Brexit and feel rooted in their community and nation and are proud of both. Who can they vote for? Whereas if you're an affluent, secular, metropolitan liberal, you have three main parties anxious for your vote."

There is a need for a party that represents decent, aspirational, patriotic hard-working people, struggling to move forward with their lives. Struggling to achieve security for themselves and their children. Many of these people are likely to have voted Leave. They are not concerned about doctrine, or platforming, they are concerned about practical steps that will improve their lives and give them confidence in the future. These people are not fighting a class war. They want to be wealthy themselves. They are more concerned about the people they live alongside. Those that need help. But also, those they see playing the system; taking without giving. Those that are unruly, that spoil their lives with crime and anti-social behaviour with no apparent sanction or control.

The Labour party and the unions have left these people behind. The Conservative party no longer understand them. The Liberal Democratic party will always be too middle class. There is a gap to be filled. These people need a voice in parliament, even if that voice offends liberal sensitivities. If our political system were working properly, a party like this would emerge. A party with policies that are explicit and well thought out, clearly not racist or discriminatory, and capable of being put into effect once in power. It could be that the "*Brexit Party*" turns into this party, but very careful navigation will be required. There is the potential for all sorts of banana skins.

Organisational design

To achieve change will require four new organisations.

- An IT company to build software that will facilitate the online development of policies, from concept and discussion, to the draft legislation required to enact them.
- An organisation that will work with political parties and organisations to agree a constitutional reform agenda based around a charter of demands.
- A *Modern Political Union* that will promote this charter.
- A political comparison website that will be used by voters to compare the policies and values of parties and candidates at elections.

A system for policy debate and production

A policy production system will facilitate wide debate and consideration of policies - from conception, through to the draft legislation to enact them. A parallel is Wikipedia, a huge free to use Wiki-based system where non-paid experts work together to organise and to make available the world's knowledge. A system like this could be used to help the Royal Commission review of the NHS proposed earlier in the book. It could be made available to political parties to help them to craft better policies. The Blunders of our Governments notes that a considerable proportion of blunders might have been avoided if pre-legislation scrutiny had been a matter of routine instead of a special event. A system like this could make that happen.

How could the development of such a system be funded? There is a good parallel in the insurance industry. This comes through an industry-owned, not-for-profit company called Polaris. In the 1990s insurance products became ever more complicated, using sophisticated maths and complex rules. These products, once designed, needed to be embedded in quotation systems, often owned by third parties. Re-coding of these products was administratively costly. Errors proved very expensive because products were then sold for the wrong price. In 1993 the insurance industry decided to tackle these problems by setting up an organisation to agree common product building standards. The major insurers each invested in this company. The company then developed a common product building approach and standards, and product building software called "Product Writer". This software is now available in release 27 and is used extensively throughout the industry. This approach has largely eliminated the insurance industry's product building blunders.

A company like this could be set up and funded by individual donors on behalf of their chosen political parties or organisations. The company would develop a *Systems Infrastructure for Open Democracy* (SIFOD). This system would cut its teeth on working up the policies required to enact the Charter.

The Game Changer's Charter

The Charter Organisation will not require significant funding, but it will require significant high-profile support. Like the Magna Carta, it will need the support of powerful barons. Today's powerful barons are the people who have influence on social media. People who have wealth and contacts and are accustomed to making things happen. Journalists that can suspend their cynicism and believe that a better way is possible. Politicians that have the courage and the strength of will to take on their parties. The original Magna Carta included the names of 25 barons. That seems like a good starting threshold for launching an organisation like this. If some of those modern barons actually are barons, all the better.

A Modern Political Union

In Chapter Three, Disruption, the features of a Modern Political Union are described, as are the stages required for its development. If a project like CTG gets traction, a constitution and articles of association would need to be prepared. Key features would be a governance board, a membership policy, agreed values, a policy board (using "Pirate type" online member polls) and a code of conduct.

An organisation like this would need premises and an executive. Support would need to be provided to each of a "shadow cabinet" of policy experts. The build of a website and smartphone app would require careful architecture and project management. Regular liaison would be required with the Electoral Commission and with the *SIFOD* and *Charter* organisations. Policy friendly organisations and pressure groups would need to be kept informed of progress.

This would be an ambitious undertaking. Crowd sourcing and membership fees could have a place in funding an organisation like this, but initially, it would need independent funding. That might not be hard to obtain if the venture is seen as potentially setting up a social media platform for those that want to discuss and contribute to political policy formation. A place to direct those annoying friends of ours on Facebook that keep banging on about politics, whereas all we want to do is share pictures of our cats and dogs.

Political comparison sites

The final new organisations envisaged are the comparison sites to compare party manifestos and candidates. The market will demand these. It will be better to be proactive than to allow these to develop on an ad-hoc basis. A common manifesto format and a common format for candidate information will be an early output from the new Charter organisation. If Charter supporting parties agreed to produce their manifestos and candidate information in the same format - and to the same timetable – then at general elections the voting public will gravitate to sites that compare between them.

The Labour and Conservative parties will need to fall into line and provide manifesto and candidate information in the standard format, for the purpose of comparison - or risk being seen as the political dinosaurs that they possibly could become. The game will have started to change.

10

FINAL THOUGHTS

Politics and politicians are held in contempt and the necessary mixture of motives and give and take of the political process is despised. The state is burdensome and intrusive. The law is straining to adapt to new attitudes and technologies. The periphery of Britain is in revolt, malcontents abound in the elite, and relations with the continent are fraught; religious radicalism is on the rise. Is it silly to think there is a touch of 1215? A whiff of revolution in the air?

David Starkey, Magna Carta, published in 2015

When the Economist reviewed Robert Peston's book, WTF, they called it "highly predictable". They thought his policy ideas veered from "shop-worn banalities" to "flights of fancy". They thought him "delusional" for believing that a new generation of politicians with credible new ideas will emerge out of the current swamp. That might be said of this book too. But to achieve change, somebody must put themselves "out there" to promote it. They will probably be on their own for a while. They may attract ridicule. But it only takes a few people to support that change, for other people to start seeing it as not so strange after all. Then suddenly, a tipping point can emerge. What seemed strange before can appear like the most obvious thing to do. This principle is illustrated in a video by Michael Hughes. It is available on You Tube and called Leadership from a Dancing Guy. The video illustrates somebody dancing strangely on their own at a music festival. To start with, everyone just watches him, then one person from the crowd gets up and starts dancing with him, then another, then another. Eventually, the whole crowd joins in.

In writing this book, I am putting myself "out there". It is a good time in my life to do this. I am unknown in political circles, indeed in pretty much all circles. I don't have any political relationships or a political career to protect. I do not have any political baggage. And like the dancing guy, I am enjoying myself. I don't have any illusions about how much an unknown figure writing a book in their pyjamas can achieve. But I am an optimist. It just might happen that some people, some people that do have power and influence, will read this book and agree with me. Then something interesting might happen. And in British political history, interesting things do happen from time to time.

REFERENCES

Sources include:

The Times and The Sunday Times
Money Week Magazine
The Economist Magazine
The New Statesman Magazine
London Evening Standard
The Big Issue Magazine
Wikipedia
HistoryHome.co.uk - Dr Marjorie Bloy
The House of Commons website: Parliament.uk
The Electoral Commission - ElectoralCommission.org.uk
Office for National Statistics (ONS)
The Icelandic Pirate Party - Piratar.is
Politics – Aristotle – Baker translation
Magna Carter - David Starkey
Perilous Question – The Great Reform Bill 1832 – Antonia Fraser
Shooting Niagara - The Second Reform Act 1867 – Robert Saunders
Victorious Century – UK 1800 – 1906, David Cannadine
The English Constitution – Walter Bagehot – 1872 edition
The Will of The People – Albert Weale
Berlin Rules – Paul Lever
The Road to Somewhere – David Goodhart
The Blunders of our Governments – Anthony King & Ivor Crewe
The People Vs. Democracy – Yascha Mounk
The End of Alchemy – Mervyn King
When the Money Runs Out, Stephen King
The Limits to Growth – Club of Rome
Small is Beautiful – EF Schumacher
Progress for a Small Planet – Barbara Ward

THE GAME CHANGER'S CHARTER

Reform election rules

- Election manifestos produced to a common agreed format and timetable
- Election manifestos agreed in advance by party vote
- Revised Electoral Commission election spending rules
- On-line voting
- State political funding, based on membership numbers and votes cast

English devolution

- Devolve power to nine English kingdoms
- Establish a new English Witan to advise Parliament on English issues

Reduce the voting age

- Reduce the voting age to 16
- Establish citizenship study in schools, resulting in a reduced voting age of 14

Change the voting system

- A separate vote for party and for constituency candidate using the Additional List system, with list allocations made in proportion to party vote

- Reduce the number of MPs in Parliament to 550: 400 from constituencies, 150 from the list

Reform the House of Lords

- Reduce the number of members to 250
- 136 elected representatives from the counties
- 114 appointed roles, chosen formulaically from those that have held high office
- Responsibilities to be reframed to focus on non-executive oversight of Government
- Responsible for establishing a visible and fair honours system
- Responsible for producing annual national accounts
- All inherited titles to lapse, other than the monarchy

Modernise the Monarchy

- Agreed retirement dates for our next three kings
- Responsible for an annual *King's Survey* on national wellbeing
- Chair of K12 meetings of the UK's 12 regional leaders – which will focus on national and regional wellbeing and the protection of the UK's environment.

STATISTICS

Debt

1. The Office for National Statistics (ONS) reports that the UK's National Debt at the end of March 2018 was £1,764 billion, which represents 85.8% of GDP. This excludes off balance sheet items such as pension obligations which increases it to £3,500 billion, about 191% of GDP.

3. The National Debt Clock website estimates a higher current overall debt of £4,800 billion, equating to a debt of £78,000 per person in the UK.

4. We borrowed £43 billion in the year to 31 March 2018. (ONS)

5. We spend £50 billion a year to service our national debt.

6. We have the fourth largest debt compared to GDP of all 28 advanced economies.

Tax

7. UK tax was 33.2% of GDP in 2016. This was higher than the USA, Canada and Australia, but lower than France 45.3%, Belgium 44.2% and Denmark 45.9%.

8. The total cost of pension tax relief was £41bn for 2017/18. This was made up of £24bn of income tax relief and £17bn of NI relief on employers' contributions. This total is an increase of £1bn when compared to the previous financial year. More than 50% of this relief goes to those earning above £50,000.

Trade

9. The overall trade in goods balance widened from a £14.7 billion deficit in 1998 to a £130.7 billion deficit in 2017 in real terms. (ONS)

10. From 1998 to 2000 the UK had an average £3.5 billion trade in goods surplus with the EU. In 2001 the surplus turned into a deficit and by 2017 the trade balance with the EU was £93.7 billion in deficit, with most EU countries contributing to the deficit. (ONS)

Foreign aid

11. The UK spends 0.7% of its Gross National Income in foreign aid every year. That compares with spending in 2017 of 0.17% for the USA, 0.43% for France, 0.23% for Japan and 0.26% for Canada.

Population

12. In mid-2017 there were 55.6m people in England, 5.4m in Scotland, and 3.1m in Wales. This made a GB population of 64m. Add on Northern Ireland's 1.9m people to get a UK total of 65.9m. (ONS). This total has grown by 8.9m since 1975.

13. The UN estimates the UK's population to be 67m in 2019. This figure is forecast to grow to 69.2m by 2026, with England growing fastest – up by 5.9% between mid-2016 to mid-2026 (ONS).

14. The UK has 694 people per square mile, compared with France at 306 and the USA at 86. England is the second most densely populated region in the EU, with 410 people per square KM, behind Holland with 497 people. That compares with Germany at 229 and France at 121.

15. The English population has grown by 4.3 million in the past decade. London's population has increased by 1.7 million

(more than 25%) since 1997. It is eight times larger than the next largest city in Britain.

17. Until the mid-1990's Britain had never had gross migration inflows of over 300,000, but since the mid-2000's the annual inflows have never been below 500,000. Current ONS projections assume inward migration of 5.4 million in the decade to 2028.

18. Current global population of 7.7 bn is expected to reach 8.6 bn in 2030, 9.6 bn in 2050 and 11.2 bn in 2100.

19. Africa's population is expected to double from 1.26 bn last year to 2.53 bn in 2050, making it the most populous continent in the world.

20. Nigeria has the fastest growing population of the ten most densely populated countries of the world and is set to overtake the US as the third most populous country on the planet before 2050.

21. According to the World Wildlife Fund, by 2025 two thirds of the world's population will face potential water shortages.

Politics

22. In 2013 membership of the three main Westminster parties hit an all-time low of 0.8% of the population.

23. Britain makes up 12.9% of the EU's population, but just 2.8% of European Commission staff and 2.4% of European Council staff.

24. The EU referendum in 2016 resulted in 17.4m votes for Leave and 16.1m votes for Remain. 406 constituencies voted to Leave and 242 to Remain. In Labour held constituencies 148 voted to Leave and 84 voted to Remain. In Conservative held constituencies 247 voted to Leave and 80 voted to Remain. Nine UK regions voted to leave and three voted to Remain. In Parliament, 160 MPs support

Leave and 486 MPs support Remain.

Education

26. The OECD reported in 2016 that Britain had the lowest literary rate and the second lowest numeracy rate of the 23 richest countries.

27. Seventeen percent of people still leave British schools functionally illiterate, and 22% functionally innumerate.

QUOTATIONS AND EXTRACTS

Political re-alignment

Rachel Sylvester: "A political definition of loyalty that requires MPs to vote against their consciences, a party system that forces people into old-fashioned boxes, a model of leadership that mitigates against emotional honesty, surely cannot survive in the age of individuality."

Niall Ferguson: "The old coalition between progressive elites and the proletariat is broken. The former is too liberal on immigration, too in love with multiculturalism. The latter loathe both."

Caitlin Moran: "For the first time in my adult life, I don't know who to vote for. I spend an hour oscillating between the Greens and the Women's Equality Party. Which of these two parties, who will never get into power, shall I gift my essentially useless vote to, during these times of unprecedented democratic crisis?"

Populism

Kingsley Chiedu Moghal, "A borderless world diminishes the voices of local populations and amplifies the powers of bureaucratic global elites. Large populations in industrial nations find themselves on the wrong side of globalisation's inescapable logic as cheap foreign labour and technology destroys their jobs. Populism seeks to reverse the power of the international community by using the democratic legitimacy of the majority to reassert primacy of national interest. A dismissive response only leaves us unable to manage the implications for democracy."

David Goodhart, "Shorn of the Hard Authoritarians decent populism is a fundamentally mainstream world view representing a large part of the centre ground of British politics. Large majorities reject mass immigration, place a high value on national citizenship, are hostile to much non-contributory welfare, and do not like modern multiculturalism (at least in its separatist form). It is in this overlapping majority that "decent populism" is to be found."

Professor Diomidis Spinellis, "Being able to buy a Chinese-made 50-inch TV when you work by flipping hamburgers for the minimum wage may be more efficient than working in a factory on wages where you can only afford the 30-inch American-made model. But Donald Trump's voters weighed up factors that many economists and your newspaper (The Economist) often downplay: the marginal utility of consumer goods in a rich society, the distribution of wealth and a sense of self-worth."

Migration

Stephen King, "Increasingly western voters are rejecting a world of open borders in which goods, capital, and importantly people, can move without serious impediment."

Roger Bootle: "Government should have a policy for population which needs to be integrated with policies for housing and transport. We have had the very opposite of joined-up government – totally open borders, a messed-up policy on residential housing, and a rubbish transport policy. Disaster. We need to think about what sort of numbers we think are reasonable for Britain to accommodate."

Victor Orban, "I do not want to see the country drifting towards a situation where lower-skilled work would only be carried out by foreigners. We ourselves have to do the work required to keep our economy going, from scrubbing toilets to nuclear science."

Max Hastings, "Today's waves of African migration are merely a prelude. Of the 2.2bn citizens added to the global population by 2050, 1.3bn will be Africans – about the size of China's population today. And more of them will have means of travel, since it is as they get wealthier that people obtain the ability to plan and to pay for travel. As African countries gradually prosper, migration will surely increase, not decrease."

Stephen Smith, "Europe should become more engaged with individual

African countries and trade blocks, building regulated routes for migrants travelling in both directions".

Peter Richards, "The homelessness figures for this Christmas are shocking. In my youth, I never saw a beggar in Britain: now rough sleepers are everywhere. This is what an endless supply of cheap workers has brought us. It has done immense damage to the value of labour and the ordinary people of this country."

Finance and taxation

Mervyn King, "Monetary stimulus via low interest rates works largely by giving incentives to bring forward spending from the future to the present. As time passes, we will be digging larger and larger holes in future demand... Today's extraordinarily low interest rates discourage savings – the source of future demand – and if maintained indefinitely, will pull down rates of return on investment, diverting resources into unprofitable projects. Both effects will drag down future growth rates."

Stephen D King, "If a country's creditors no longer trust governments and the myopic taxpayers who vote for those governments, the creditors will "asset strip" Western nations, leaving generations to come without the assets – including real estate and companies – that nurtured and sustained previous generations. Companies and their bespoke technologies will slowly fall under foreign ownership, turning the US and the UK into nations of worker bees where the profits of their endeavours head overseas It is hardly an appealing prospect. It's what happens when you continuously try to live beyond your means."

Victoria Bischoff, "The top savings rate for individuals is still pretty pathetic, but it won't get better unless the government acts. It is still borrowing around £40bn a year. Couldn't it shift the balance, so it borrows more from the nations savers and flogs fewer government bonds to the markets?"

John Frew, ex md of Weir Group, "Scotland's demographics going forward are absolutely horrible. The working population between the ages of 16 and 65 will fall dramatically in the next 10 years. This can only represent a huge fall in our GDP and tax collected…. Most intelligent young people I know have already moved south and I can only see this increasing to a stampede."

Defence

Economist, "A swarm of small military drones might be released into a theatre of operations, spread out to look for targets and then collectively assign tasks to different drones within the swarm. When one target has been destroyed the swarm can move on to another. But this type of weapon will encounter cultural resistance from military types who want to retain a role for human pilots and traditional aircraft. Tanks faced similar objections in the first world war when they were initially seen merely as an adjunct to infantry."

Freedom

Mark Littlewood, Institute of Economic Affairs: "If we are serious about becoming a progressive country, we should take a leading role in ending the war on drugs. A policy approach that would improve health outcomes, enable savings in the police budget, stifle organised crime, and enhance tax revenues should command widespread support. But most politicians remain unwilling to properly discuss the issue. This is even though the empirical and economic evidence for decoupling drug use from the criminal law is overwhelming."

Melanie Reid: "A kindly final act by a devoted partner will lead to prosecution, and maybe prison. This is utterly inhumane. Criminal punishment or mercy killing, or assisted suicide, is one of the great iniquities on the statute book – made, protected and enforced by people who don't have a scooby about the reality of living with extreme illness, suffering or disability. It is able-bodied, sanctimonious law guarded by misplaced religiosity, not humanity."

Hunter Adams, retired doctor and former health minister of Guernsey: "It's not about doctors. It's not about churchgoers. It's about what people want when they are coming to the end of their lives."

The Economist, "International law recognises no right to self-determination by a region in an advanced democracy. No serious

European politician is willing to countenance this. Britain's referendum on Scottish independence is unlikely to be copied elsewhere."

Europe

Professor Robert Tombs, "The Remain vote rests on several beliefs. The first is the belief that European integration represents progress – the supersession of nation states by an international order. The second is that Britain is a nation in decline, incapable of flourishing outside the EU. The third is that the lower classes are unqualified to make big political choices and are infected with reactionary ideas and habits."

Alice Thompson, "This country is re-evaluating itself and may be going through a period of introspection, but I am beginning to feel optimistic, as is most of the population. Happiness ratings have risen in the past year, according to the Office for National Statistics."

Mervyn King, "Monetary union has created a conflict between a centralised elite on the one hand, and the forces of democracy at the national level on the other. This is extraordinarily dangerous. This approach of creeping transfer of sovereignty to an unelected centre is deeply flawed and will meet popular resistance."

David Goodhart, "When people in Sunderland voted for Brexit apparently against their material interests it was considered stupid; when affluent people vote for higher taxes it is considered admirable."

Julie Burchill, "Against the orders of our betters, we oiks reclaimed our democracy and were practically delirious with the joy of insurrection. We find ourselves quite at odds with those Remainers often with a Polish au pair and a second home in Provence – who took to Facebook to work themselves up into a mass hysteria rivalled only by the Strasbourg dancing plague of 1518: "Esme and Arlo hugged me this morning , tears running down their little faces – and asked "Why have the bad people stolen our future , Mummy?" and "Where will all the avocados come from after Brexit – tell me that!!""

Am buying up tinned meat."

Paul Lever, "In 2014 Jean-Claude Juncker was elected Commission president. Nobody in Britain voted for him. He was opposed by David Cameron, and all of the main British political parties. He did not receive the support of a single British member of the European Parliament."

National Planning

Roger Bootle, "What really matter are questions of emotion, motivation, identity and institutions. Mancur Olson wrote that the secret to a successful country is having the elites and their presumptions and institutions turned over every so often, which we never have – Britain coasted through much of the post-war period because, as it were, we had won. Look at Singapore. When it came out of the Malaysia Federation, it was up against it. So, it made some tough decisions, which were extremely well followed through."

Sarah Gordon. "Fast and reliable Wi-Fi is a utility, like electricity, and a modern economy must have a long-term policy to provide it to all business and households in order to remain globally competitive. Many of our regions have dreadful internet services. Government investment to bring fast and reliable internet to them would provide more benefits than HS2."

Adam Minter, "A scooter with a detachable, switchable battery is being developed, but ultimately the switch to e-vehicles will need the support of governments. Standardising batteries, charging stations and regulations that focus on reducing pollution are the key priorities now."

Warren East, CEO of Rolls-Royce: "It is very disappointing, and a missed opportunity, that ministers have not embraced RR's Small Modular Reactor technology (SMR) to build mini-nuclear power stations. We have talked about it as an export opportunity. If we can't rely on the British Government and that means we build SMR's outside of the UK, that's a loss to the UK."

Community

Aristotle, "While a city comes into existence for the sake of mere life, it exists for the sake of a good life."

David Goodhart, "In recent years there has been a "rights disconnect": a declining willingness of those called up to fund, through their taxes, the rights of others. Redistribution requires a sense of shared citizenship and national community."

Alice Thompson, "When done well, local sourcing helps to build communities, protect the environment and gives shoppers the satisfaction of knowing the provenance of food or craftmanship."

Suranga Herath, CEO, English Tea Shop, "Our business is rooted in sustainability. We believe businesses should be savvy about how long-term growth can be achieved across the supply chain. Businesses nowadays have more of a responsibility to go beyond profit-making only models and to use their influence to better the wider community."

Julian Manley, "If there are opportunities for making a success of life in Preston, a place where people have a sense of identity and belonging, then social capital is potentially increased: pride of place is enhanced; a sense of citizenship is developed; and democracy becomes relevant and vital."

Aristotle, "Goodness by itself is not enough: there must also be a capacity for being active in doing good."

David Goodhart, "Ambition and the pursuit of success are perfectly decent human impulses, but most people know that being valued is more important than being successful."

Education

Meryn Somerset-web, "It is not old age that is getting longer, it is middle age. This has obvious social implications. We need to encourage systems where people can dial in and out of education over a lifetime and are better able to change careers, and hence find ways to let even those in their 80's to be productive, valued members of society. This sounds simple but in fact adds up to a complete reshaping of the world as we know it."

David Goodhart, "Rather than invest more in universities ... the government would be better advised to invest more in part time further education and stepping stone para-professional jobs – such as teaching assistants or police support staff – which can give people a second chance to get on a decent career ladder."

Development Aid

Jeremy Warner, "China's hugely ambitious Belt and Road Initiative is an enlightened piece of forward thinking routed in the idea of development, trade and infrastructure as a mutual, holistic benefit. Too much of our Western aid is spent on virtue signalling. Well directed development spending today promises to save us from all manner of problems in the future."

John Bird, Founder of The Big Issue, "I am trying to invent a philosophy of dismantling poverty, rather than simply keeping the poor comfortable. And a science of New Government. To stop the crass waste of money that sees spending on problems after they have become a problem: and not before they have become a problem. All little things should coalesce into a Big Plan. They should help a big goal. And the big goal must be, to end the tyranny of homelessness. Using trade, not aid, to aid people out of grief is our mantra."

Gerry Anderson, "I started to think that there really ought to be dumps around the world with rescue gear standing by, so that when a disaster happened, all these items of rescue equipment could be rushed to the disaster zone and used to help to get people out of trouble ... I was thinking, 'Rescue, yes, rescue, but how to make it science fiction? What about an International Rescue organisation?'"

A SWOT ANALYSIS FOR THE UK

Strengths

- Favourable island location. Temperate weather. Easy access to USA, Europe, Africa and Asia
- Strong and stable democracy. Low corruption. Strong legal system and institutions
- Well-developed physical infrastructure and a strong and fascinating historical legacy
- Strong sense of national identity, good diversity and integration, positive culture
- A large economy, with some world leading industries, companies and sectors
- Well networked in the world, and big enough to have influence
- A strong national brand, many national icons, a proud history, home of the English language
- A leader in education, sporting endeavour, and the cultural and creative sectors
- Comparatively good demographic profile
- A willingness and capability to defend ourselves and to help our allies
- Self-confidence, and a belief in the brilliance of being British

Weaknesses

- Comparatively small surface area, some parts very densely populated
- Large amount of public and private debt, and a persistent current account deficit
- Large aging infrastructure, expensive to upkeep, a disadvantage against start-up economies
- Large regional imbalances

- A persistent trade deficit
- Persistent and growing disparities in wealth and opportunities
- Infrastructure not keeping up with growth in demand
- Some imbalance in industry sectors
- Poor language skills
- Overconfident, arrogant, island mentality, not good at working in alliances of equals

Opportunities

- Regional investment and development
- Better government and planning
- Better national PR and targeting, leveraging our national assets
- Forming new international alliances, strengthening existing ones
- Infrastructure investment and renewal
- Unleashing our creative and entrepreneurial spirit
- Leading the world in diversity, tolerance, and nurturing our people and environment

Threats

- Negative impacts on our environment and culture through excessive and uncontrolled growth
- Poor terms of trade following Brexit
- Scottish independence, and regional dissatisfaction
- An economic crisis caused by excessive debt
- Social conflict and economic drag caused by inequality of income, wealth and opportunity
- Excessive regulation of markets and business
- Excessive costs from the needs of an aging population
- Climate change causing UK flooding & storms, and large movements of people across borders
- Global instability and conflict

BIOGRAPHY

This section records some of the influences that have helped me to form my political thinking. It also records some of the major events, political and non-political, that have happened during my lifetime.

The 1970s were a troubled time. There was a feeling of national decline. The hope for the country was North Sea Oil. Our class was asked to write essays on how we should spend our new-found financial bonanza. It would be interesting to find those essays now.

When I was 16, my school turned from a traditional boys' grammar school in Hastings, established in 1619, into a comprehensive. We had a new intake of boys. It was as difficult for them as it was for us, but some of this new intake just wouldn't do what they were told. It became difficult to work in the library.

This was an exciting time to be young. The music and the youth culture were distinctive and vibrant. But it was also a dangerous time. The cars were dangerous. The motorbikes were dangerous. The disc jockeys and the priests were dangerous. Fighting in the street was a national sport. Jo Brand recalls that Hastings was a place you'd go to if you wanted a fight. She was right, but people didn't generally get shot, they didn't generally get stabbed.

Given the amount of "going out" that went on, it is amazing that any of us got to university. But the TV only had three channels, we didn't have mobile phones or social media, and there was no Netflix. I went to UCL to study Economics and Geography. Margaret Thatcher came to power just before I went to university. I didn't know what to make of her, though I was shocked by the stridency of her message and the amount of conflict she generated. My father, a teacher, called her "Milk Snatcher Thatcher" as she had stopped the free school milk. I was concerned that my student grant was not going to be as safe as it was before.

At university, I became a Guardian reader. The "old" manufacturing industries, largely in the North, were being left to flounder. Somehow, brutal industrial carnage was supposed to be a good thing.

The lack of humanity and compassion in promoting policies that created so much unemployment and misery shocked me. Subsequently, the country regained its confidence. It became a more prosperous and a better place to live. Whether we needed such harsh medicine, I wonder. Union power did need to be confronted, but the cost was very high. At the time, the alternative was the uncompromising and unattractive brand of socialism promoted by Michael Foot.

I did not get involved with politics at university, although there was plenty of politics at UCL. There was a strong Lesbian and Gay community and an assertive form of feminism. This was a new thing for a young chap from an all boys' school in Hastings. It was a bit confusing, as was the music scene at that time. I couldn't understand the New Romantics - or persuade myself to buy the type of clothes that would get me into the Blitz Club down the road.

I enjoyed my studies, and the energy of London. I soaked in the environmental and ecological parts of my Geography course. Books like The Limits to Growth made a big impact. I realised that our world needs to be cherished. We couldn't continue to live without thought for the future. The other side of my studies was Economics. The theories of Robert Malthus, Adam Smith and Keynesian economics made an impact. Monetarism was the fashionable economic theory of the day, but that seemed like a blunt instrument to me.

I started part-time work when I reached 16. I had acquired a taste for beer and smoking, for buying music and for taking girls out. Those things required funding. I worked in Sainsbury's on Friday nights and Saturdays. Sainsbury's was a happy place. Everyone had time for a chat and to help people out. Then a new store manager arrived from out of town. He adopted the approach that we staff were lazy slackers and needed to be kicked into line. It was like Captain Bligh had arrived. I started to get the point of unions, although we didn't have one. But I will be forever grateful to Sainsbury's for one thing. I met my future wife there. I was a trolley-jockey. Caroline mainly worked on the tills. One year she had to deal with the broken Easter eggs, bagging up the broken chocolate for sale to staff. There was a suspiciously large number of these. Some of that chocolate found its way to me. Love blossomed.

In those years vacation jobs were easy to find. In my university summer breaks, I taught English to foreign students. This was a big thing in seaside towns like Hastings. I taught mainly Italians, but also Germans, and one group of Finnish students. The Finnish girls were much sought after by the Italian boys - and the attraction seemed to be mutual. I enjoyed teaching and I learned a lot. For example, I learned how to swear fluently in Italian. But teaching is responsible and demanding work that left me tired. I was happy to move to a less demanding vacation job working for the council. I helped to operate the Hastings East Hill Cliff Railway for a couple of summers. July and August were very busy, but come September, not much went on at the East Hill Lift. I got through Tolstoy's War and Peace sitting at the top of the cliff, contemplating the Up, Down and Stop buttons – while watching the sea gulls and the fishing boats. The bad part of the job was that I had to clean the public toilet at the top of the hill. But I look on my time at the East Hill Lift as the best job I have ever had.

My final year at University was 1983. Jobs were hard to find. With high unemployment, this was a difficult time for young people. Finding a first full time job is hard at any time. Young people need all the help they can get to make the first step into the world of work. I joined the accountancy firm Price Waterhouse. I started work in London, while also studying for accountancy exams. I worked harder than I had ever worked before - or have ever done since. I qualified as a chartered accountant just after London had just been through "the big bang" and was starting to do very well under the Conservatives. This was the time of the character "Loads of Money". As a young urban professional, working in the City of London, for the first time in my life I was fashionable. There was a feeling that London was starting to be the centre of everything.

In 1988 I joined Lloyd's of London. I wanted to work in an industry that produced a worthwhile product. Insurance ticked that box for me. When something goes wrong, insurance puts it right. Lloyd's had nearly destroyed itself through lax regulation. Unlimited liability membership was mis-sold to people that didn't understand it or couldn't afford it. Underwriters were exposed to a spiral of complex business that few people understood. In retrospect, the problems of Lloyd's were a harbinger of the problems to come in the banking industry.

I joined the General Review Department. This was a new regulatory unit. We were staffed by accountants and lawyers and a few market professionals. Our job was to perform site-reviews of brokers and underwriters. We took a top down approach, looking at corporate governance. We wanted to see evidence that Boards operated effectively, that there were adequate controls in place, and that the risks the business was running were properly understood and reported upon. This was the model for the FSA's later Arrow visits. Quite what crusty Lloyd's directors made of a 25-year-old quizzing them, you can guess. There was a large amount of learning on the job, but we did raise standards and improve risk control and board governance. I learned how Boards should operate. I also learned how to recognise a Masonic handshake.

During my time at Lloyd's there was rejoicing and amazement in the City when the top rate of income tax fell from 60% to 40%. This was tinged with some worry at Lloyd's that their attraction as a tax effective investment for wealthy people had reduced. The change seemed audacious and potentially divisive, but the Labour party was unattractive at that time and unable to capitalise. In retrospect, it was a brilliant move, increasing the tax take and signalling that Britain was a land where enterprise was rewarded. It attracted many high earners into the City.

On 1 January 1990, I started the new decade with a new job working in finance for NIG Skandia, an insurer on the northern fringes of the City. I spent the next 14 years at NIG. I moved from finance to operations, controlling HR, premises, service and claims handling. Then I took on responsibility for the Personal Lines business division, owning a profit and loss account for the first time. Eventually, I became managing director. I was involved with several start-ups. We established Dial Direct as a new telesales broker to sell car and home insurance. We established Finsure as a new premium finance company. I was involved with a lot of M&A activity. In my second year as managing director, NIG was voted Best Insurer Overall in the Insurance Times Awards, beating companies like Axa, Zurich and Norwich Union. That was a very proud moment.

In these years I lived in North London with Caroline. As we approached 30 and planned to start a family we decided to move to Orpington. This was closer to Hastings and our families. We got more living space for our money. The luxury of parking your car on your own drive. Orpington was a shock. From a flat on "The Ladder" off trendy Green Lanes in Haringey, to the suburban quiet of a three-bedroom semi-detached. We tried hard to find some life in the community. We joined the local church and various clubs and societies. For the first time, I joined a political party. Our income increased as we got promotions at work, but so did our costs as our mortgage interest rose. Interest rates were high to protect the value of Sterling in the European Exchange Rate Mechanism. Our house became worth substantially less than we had paid for it. As children arrived in our lives, Alice and then Edward, Caroline gave up work to look after them. Our budget became very tight.

In 1996 I became the father of twins, Elizabeth and William, doubling my family, and putting another five years onto my working life. This was the year that Tony Blair's New Labour government got into power. They arrived accompanied by the soundtrack of "Things Can Only Get Better", and things really did. The nation was ready for a change and their policies were progressive and inclusive. Most of us did well under Tony Blair. London became the capital of the world. Taxes from high City salaries and bonuses helped to fund a large expansion of state care and welfare. It seemed as though everyone was a winner. Life was good. The stock market boomed. The internet was going to change the world. We had a huge party to bring in the New Millennium. Then, on 11 September 2001, the Twin Towers fell. The party was over. Everyone will remember where they were on that day. My company, NIG, had been purchased by Churchill, the insurer with the bulldog brand. We had just finished our monthly Churchill Group Executive meeting in Bromley. Our Chairman returned and turned on the television. We watched, appalled, as the Twin Towers burned and fell. It was like watching a disaster movie, but it was really happening. The world as we had known it had changed. We had to stand firm with our friend and ally The United States. But the response was confused and overly hasty. It wasn't the Taliban that was responsible for 9-11, but the USA needed to hit back somewhere, so we joined their invasion of Afghanistan. History should have warned us about the quagmire that would become. On March 2003 we had the second Iraq war. Our involvement was justified by the "dodgy dossier" on weapons of mass destruction. We have a debt to the Americans for helping us in two world wars. We will always want to stand by them. But we are not supposed to do stuff like this. Britain is supposed to be one of the good guys.

In June of 2003, The Royal Bank of Scotland (RBS), the owner of Direct Line, announced the purchase of Churchill, owned by Credit Suisse. NIG was part of this deal. In the next nine months we experienced the rigours of an RBS due diligence - followed by a corporate restructuring to create a new group structure. It was horrible. Churchill, Direct Line and NIG became part of RBS Insurance. Fred Goodwin took a close interest in us. We experienced the RBS way of doing things. After 14 years at NIG, and with the opportunity to leave on good terms, I decided that it was the right time for me to go. I stepped off the corporate escalator at the age of 42. I took the children to school, saw more of my family, read books on British history. My time in the garden was very happy

I had been involved with a couple of successful start-ups at NIG, so I decided to use this experience to start a new internet business. With the help of some ex-colleagues, we established a new insurance broker called Affinity B2C. This business sold car insurance through the internet using brands that targeted different affinity groups. Affinity B2C was eventually merged into a business with wider ambitions; ABC Insurance. This business was sold to Liverpool Victoria (LV) in 2006. The "ABC team" was asked to manage LV's existing insurance business while also executing the ABC Insurance business plan. My part of this plan was to set up a new distribution channel and a new commercial product set. We called this business LV Broker. In the following 10 years Liverpool Victoria's general insurance business tripled in size. We were voted the UK's best insurance company in the British Insurance Awards - another very proud moment. We won many consumer awards, and consistently topped the Which? best buy tables. We had amazing staff engagement scores. But that is another story. A story for which many people must take credit.

In politics during this time decision making in the Labour government had become dysfunctional. Personalities and personal ambition were damaging good government. Public finance had become too reliant on City finance. You make it - we'll spend it. That seemed to be the policy of the day. And spend it they did. The City banking sector helped to fund an expensive expansion of the welfare state. During this time the country continued to build up debt, at a time when it should have been paying it back. Then came the banking collapse. Lines of people waiting to withdraw money from Northern Rock. Who would have thought that we would see a run on a bank? Could things really be this bad? Yes, indeed they were, as one event after another proved. We had to confront the possibility that money in the bank might not be safe.

Insurance companies came out of the financial crisis well, but we were lumped in with banks as part of a problem that needed to be solved. We endured "intrusive regulation". We also had to adopt new EU derived regulations such as Solvency 2 and gender neutrality. In May 2010 Gordon Brown's Labour party was replaced by the more polished and consensual David Cameron - in coalition with the Nick Clegg's Liberal Democrats. David Cameron was then elected with a Conservative majority on 7 May 2015. It was clear to me that David Cameron's policy agenda was not well thought out. I started to think about how we got to this situation and how things could be done better. I started to plan this book.

The ABC team spent 2016 moving our executive responsibilities to our successors. My successor was in place early, so I had time to develop my ideas for CTG and to discuss these with some of my colleagues. A date for an EU referendum was set for 23 June 2016. David Cameron commenced a negotiation with our European partners. There were important issues to raise, but the negotiation turned into a botched, rushed, and humiliating process. Yet it didn't have to be that way. The EU needs to change. If we had worked to form alliances, worked up a common agenda and timetable for change, we could have developed a new type of relationship for those countries not using the Euro. We could have done this while staying within the EU and using our influence to help reform to happen. But it wasn't to be.

After we left LV, my ABC colleagues and I set up ABC Investors. This is a partnership that invests in early start up technology companies, mostly in Fintech. Together, we have made over 30 investments. We have seen many interesting technology propositions. This has been a good way to understand what new technology can achieve, while moving to a portfolio career with more time for personal projects. CTG has been one of these.

Change-The-Game.uk

Recent events are well known. The dysfunction in government has been shocking to behold. The EU exit negotiations have been handled very badly. Britain has lost international prestige and respect. Uncertainty is everywhere. Our political parties are divided. Our MPs have been found wanting. Our political processes are broken. None of our political parties has a compelling plan for our future...... Something has to be done about it.

You've read the book, now have your say.

Do you agree that our political system needs to change?

If candidates and parties signed up to a common
agenda for political reform, would you be more likely to vote for
them?

If the answer to these questions is yes, let your voice be heard.

Register your support

Visit the website:
change-the-game.uk

Follow us on social media:

@AModernBritain   @AModernBritain   Change The Game UK

Printed in Poland
by Amazon Fulfillment
Poland Sp. z o.o., Wrocław

49988567R00115